Winning LEGO MINDSTORMS Programming

James J. Trobaugh
Mannie Lowe

Apress*

Winning LEGO MINDSTORMS Programming

ISBN-13 (pbk): 978-1-4302-4536-0

ISBN-13 (electronic): 978-1-4302-4537-7

President and Publisher: Paul Manning
Lead Editor: Jonathan Gennick
Technical Reviewers: Mannie Lowe and Mark Edelman
Editorial Board: Steve Anglin, Ewan Buckingham, Gary Cornell, Louise Corrigan, Morgan Ertel, Jonathan
    Gennick, Jonathan Hassell, Robert Hutchinson, Michelle Lowman, James Markham, Matthew Moodie,
    Jeff Olson, Jeffrey Pepper, Douglas Pundick, Ben Renow-Clarke, Dominic Shakeshaft, Gwenan Spearing,
    Matt Wade, Tom Welsh
Coordinating Editor: Mark Powers
Copy Editor: Kimberly Burton-Weisman
Compositor: SPi Global
Indexer: SPi Global
Artist: SPi Global
Cover Designer: Anna Ishchenko

Distributed to the book trade worldwide by Springer Science+Business Media New York, 233 Spring Street, 6th Floor, New York, NY 10013. Phone 1-800-SPRINGER, fax (201) 348-4505, e-mail orders-ny@springer-sbm.com, or visit www.springeronline.com.

For information on translations, please e-mail rights@apress.com, or visit www.apress.com.

Apress and friends of ED books may be purchased in bulk for academic, corporate, or promotional use. eBook versions and licenses are also available for most titles. For more information, reference our Special Bulk Sales-eBook Licensing web page at www.apress.com/bulk-sales.

Any source code or other supplementary materials referenced by the author in this text is available to readers at www.apress.com/9781430245360. For detailed information about how to locate your book's source code, go to www.apress.com/source-code.

Contents at a Glance

Contents

About the Authors

James J. Trobaugh is an experienced coach and leader in the FIRST LEGO League. He is author of the acclaimed book Winning Design! (Apress, 2010), which focuses on the physical aspects of LEGO MINDSTORMS robot design. James has been involved with the FIRST LEGO League since 2004 as coach for Team Super Awesome, and as a technical judge at LEGO World Festival. He is also the FIRST LEGO League Director of the Forsyth Alliance in Forsyth County, Georgia.

James started out as a LEGO hobbyist. He founded the North Georgia LEGO Train Club in 1998. He finds LEGO robotics to be a natural blending of his LEGO hobby and his day job as a software architect. An added bonus is the joy of sharing his love of technology not only with his own children, but with kids in general.

Mannie Lowe is currently the FIRST program manager for the Center for Mathematics and Science Education at the University of Mississippi. He is responsible for the FIRST Tech Challenge (FTC) program for Mississippi, having held these same responsibilities in Georgia the previous seven years. Mannie is a firm believer in the mission of FIRST and how it can impact students into a better way of life. He has coached and mentored several FTC, FIRST Robotics Competition (FRC), and FIRST LEGO League (FLL) teams to award-winning seasons.

Mannie acts as a resource to many other coaches and mentors throughout the country. He is a partner in YES!—Youth Engaged in Science, a Georgia-based educational enrichment program that teaches engaging, hands-on technology programs for children of all ages using robotics, science, mathematics, and computers. Mannie is passionate about providing opportunities for kids to move into engineering, science, and technical education on the way to careers that will improve the lives of all.

About the Technical Reviewer

Mark Edelman is program director and cofounder of the nonprofit Playing At Learning. Playing At Learning coordinates the Junior FIRST LEGO League, the FIRST LEGO League, and the FIRST Tech Challenge programs for Northern California. Mark is active in Northern California youth robotics, having coached and mentored Botball, FIRST LEGO League, FIRST Tech Challenge, and FIRST Robotics teams. He is an advocate for hands-on learning programs, particularly those structured around engineering, technology, and experimentation.

Acknowledgments

A project such as this book always relies on many different people to make it happen and finish on time.

I would like to thank Jonathan Gennick and Mark Powers at Apress for giving me the chance to work on this book and for gently pushing me along as needed to meet deadlines. Their confidence in my work and encouragement has made writing this book enjoyable.

Also, I would like to give special thanks to Mannie Lowe, who started out as the technical reviewer for the book, but then stepped in and wrote some chapters as well. Mannie's knowledge and commitment to LEGO robotics is greatly appreciated. He shows his dedication to detail throughout the book.

Thanks to Mark Edelman for taking over as technical reviewer mid-project. It was nice that he could come into the project and quickly get up to speed without hesitation. His notes were always helpful and well thought out.

Special thanks to my family for putting up with me while I pushed to meet deadlines. And thanks to my children for being test subjects for many of my sample solutions and for modeling for a few of the pictures included in the book.

—James J. Trobaugh

Introduction

A robot is only as good as the instructions that it's given. Even the best-designed robots need clear and concise instructions to perform at their best. With the knowledge in this book, you will be able to expand your programming skills, as well as avoid many of the common pitfalls that NXT-G software writers fall into.

Who This Book Is For

This book is for individuals or teams that compete in any LEGO robotics competitions. The techniques covered in this book are intended to build upon a reader's existing basic NXT-G skill set. In this book, the entire program development process is covered—from brainstorming, to logic flow, and then finally to the actual writing of the code. All of these steps are important.

You will also find many examples of useful code for making the most of your robot's sensors and motors. Each of the sensors is addressed using real-world competition scenarios that give examples of how you can make your robot's program effective in completing the necessary missions.

Many coders find the basics of NXT-G easy to pick up on their own, but then struggle to learn the more advanced ideas that can be the difference between a good robot and a winning robot. The tips and methods explained in this book will help give any team the edge it needs at an event.

How This Book Is Structured

Chapters 1 and 2 introduce the NXT-G development environment and the design process we recommend when writing code.

Chapters 3 through 6 cover some key topics that help you take your code to the next level and write competition-quality programs. You'll learn about modularizing with My Blocks, about debugging and troubleshooting when things go wrong, how to move data efficiently, and generally how to make good decisions in designing your programs.

Chapters 7 through 10 detail each of the input sensors and motors that your NXT-G code will be interacting with as it attempts to complete various missions. The examples start out simple and then build in complexity to help you better understand the concepts that make the most of each available input and output device.

The final chapters cover complex code management and useful tips and tricks that can benefit any NXT-G programmer—not only in competitions but generally anytime anyone wishes to develop advanced skills for working with the LEGO MINDSTORMS system.

Supplementary Downloads

For those of you who have purchased the black and white print version of this book, we've made the color versions of each image available for download from the book's apress.com webpage, which can be found at www.apress.com/9781430245360. Just click on the Source Code/Downloads tab, which will reveal the download link.

Meeting the NXT-G Software

Let me introduce you to the LEGO MINDSTORMS programming software, NXT-G. Over the course of this book we are going to work closely with NXT-G to develop programs for your LEGO MINDSTORMS robot, so take some time to familiarize yourself with the NXT-G programming environment.

But before you do that, you need to understand what a "program" is. A program is a set of electronic instructions that are given to a computer to tell it what to do. In your case, the LEGO MINDSTORMS NXT brick is your computer, and it needs to hear from you what you want it to do and how you want it to perform a task. Your program will give the NXT a list of instructions to follow that will tell it exactly how you want it to act and respond.

The NXT-G graphical approach to programming allows you to create these instructions quickly and in a format that you, as a human, can understand. Once your program is completed, it will be translated into a language format that the NXT can understand. We will cover this process later in this chapter.

Flavors of NXT-G

NXT-G has been around since 1998, but, just like you, it has grown significantly, becoming bigger and smarter. There are a few different versions of NXT-G available, but they all do the same thing—translate programs for the LEGO MINDSTORMS NXT.

Currently there are two versions of the NXT-G software available, NXT-G 2.0 Retail, which comes with the retail LEGO MINDSTORMS kits, and NXT-G 2.1 Educational version, which is available from LEGO Education. Both versions include similar functionality, and the lessons in this book apply to each.

Note Screen shots shown in this book of NXT-G will be from NXT-G 2.1 LEGO MINDSTORMS Education version. Your screens could look different if you are using a different version of NXT-G. To find the latest version of the NXT-G software available, check the LEGO MINDSTORMS website.

The User Interface

When you start the NXT-G software, you will be presented with a graphical environment for creating your programs; this is called the User Interface, or UI. Here you will see a variety of panels designed to help you create your program (Figure 1-1). Let's review the panels individually to get a better understanding of what they do for you.

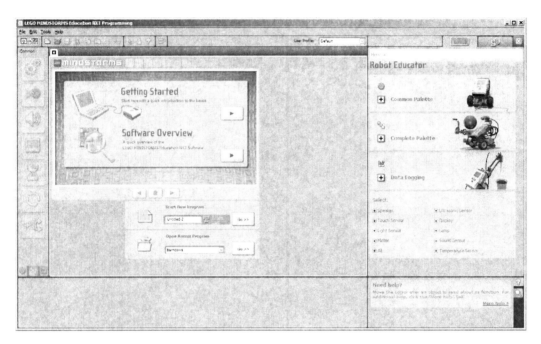

Figure 1-1. NXT-G Software User Interface when first started

Startup Panel

The Startup Panel (Figure 1-2) has quick-start buttons for creating new programs or accessing programs you've worked on recently. The panel also includes access to some basic NXT-G tutorials.

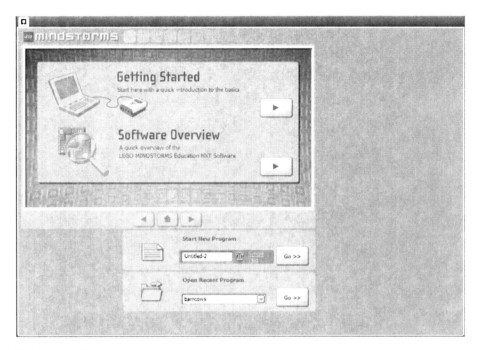

Figure 1-2. NXT-G User Interface startup panel

Program Block Palettes

Program blocks are what we use to create our NXT-G programs. The blocks include instructions on how our NXT should act—everything from moving, checking sensors, making sounds, and displaying information on the NXT screen.

Think of blocks as your tools and the palette area as your toolbox, a place where you keep all your blocks sorted and organized.

The block palettes are divided into three sections: Common blocks, Complete blocks, and Custom blocks. The three tabs at the bottom of the palette area allow you to switch among the various palettes.

Common Palette

Our Common palette (Figure 1-3) includes seven blocks, five of which you'll make good use of throughout further chapters. These are blocks that you will find yourself going to again and again. It's nice to have them in their own palette so that you can find them quickly without having to do much searching around.

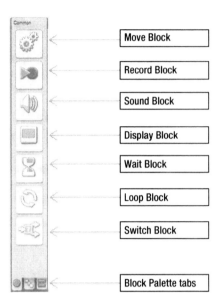

Figure 1-3. Common block palette

The five blocks from this palette that you'll use most often are the Move, Display, Wait, Loop, and Switch. Don't worry if you don't know the purposes of these blocks at this time; we'll cover each in more detail in future chapters.

Complete Palette

The Complete palette (Figure 1-4) offers six different palettes that have blocks organized by the type of functionality they offer: Common, Action, Sensor, Flow, Data, and Advanced.

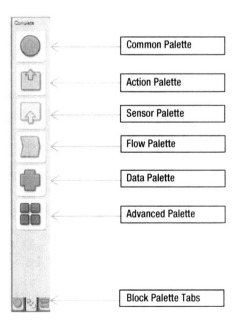

Figure 1-4. Complete block palette

Just based on their names, you get a good idea of what kinds of blocks are associated with each palette. As we progress and learn more about writing programs, we'll cover many of the blocks found in each of these palettes.

Custom Palette

Custom Palette (Figure 1-5) is just what the name implies. This is where you can store any blocks you have created yourself, My Blocks, or any blocks you have downloaded from the Internet. My Blocks is an important concept that we will study very shortly; the idea is that you can take any program you have written and create your own NXT-G block so that you can reuse the program without having to rewrite the same code. This can save time and memory on your NXT.

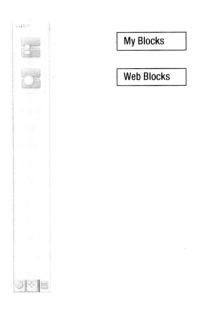

Figure 1-5. Custom block palette

Worksheet Panel

The Worksheet panel is the area in the center of the screen (Figure 1-6). Here is where you will work with your blocks and actually develop your NXT-G program. The tabs across the top allow you to switch among different programs, and the square tab to the far left will return you to the Start-Up panel that you saw when you first started the NXT-G program interface.

Figure 1-6. *Worksheet panel*

In the Worksheet panel, you will find the sequence beam that you will build your program along. The program blocks will be put in the order of how you want them to run.

Properties Panel

In the Properties panel you will be able to alter and adjust properties of your program blocks (Figure 1-7). Each block will have unique properties, so the look of this panel will change based on which block is selected in your current program.

Figure 1-7. *Properties panel with the Move block properties displayed*

Help Panel

If you have questions about any of the programming blocks, you can simply point to the block with your mouse and the Help panel will show a short description about the block and its use. For more detailed information, click on "More help>" link to open an extensive help file for the selected block. You can see an example of the help supplied for the Move block in Figure 1-8.

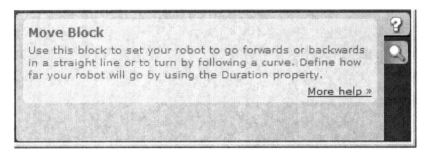

Figure 1-8. Help Panel displaying help for the Move block

Robot Educator

The Robot Educator as seen in Figure 1-9 (or Robo Center in the retail NXT-G version) gives you lots of sample robot designs and code. This is a good place for the beginner to learn some basics of NXT-G. I would encourage you to look through what is offered here and try some of the projects out for yourself. You can close this panel to give yourself more space in the Worksheet Panel by clicking on the "X" in the upper-right-hand corner.

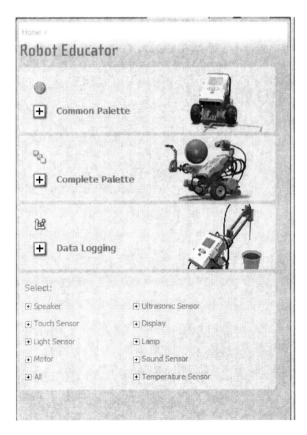

Figure 1-9. Robot Educator panel

Map Panel

Using the Map panel (Figure 1-10) is a great way to navigate around large programs. Often you can create an NXT-G program that exceeds the viewable space in the Worksheet panel,and the Map panel will let you scroll quickly around your fill Worksheet area and make finding a particular part of your much easier.

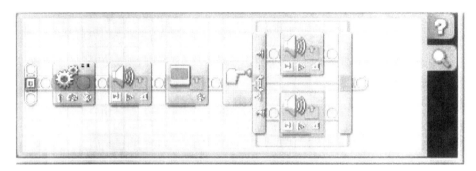

Figure 1-10. Map panel

Controller

The Controller, as seen in Figure 1-11, lives in the lower right corner of your Worksheet panel. This is what you will use to communicate and control your NXT brick. Most important, you will establish the connection to your NXT brick with the controller as well as download your program to the NXT. Later chapters examine the Controller in more detail.

Figure 1-11. The Controller

Toolbar

The toolbar (Figure 1-12) lives at the top of the user interface. It gives fast access to many of the common functions you will use frequently while working with your programs.

Figure 1-12. Toolbar

Connecting the NXT

There are two options for connecting your MINDSTORMS NXT brick to your computer and the NXT-G software, USB cable, and wireless Bluetooth. Each has advantages and disadvantages, depending on your situation.

USB

Connecting the NXT to the computer with the USB cable is the simplest method. It simply requires you to connect the cable to the USB port on the NXT brick and then to an open USB port on your computer. The first time you do this, you will be prompted to install a MINDSTORMS NXT driver for your operating system. If this does not happen automatically, you can find the necessary drivers on your software install disk.

The limitation is that your NXT brick must be tethered to the computer every time you wish to download a new or revised program. This can be inconvenient if your computer is not located close to the area where you are working with your robot.

Bluetooth

Setting up Bluetooth communication between your computer and the NXT brick can be tricky at times. I will explain the steps in getting Bluetooth enabled on the NXT but suggest that you consult your computer's manufacturer for information on how to enable Bluetooth on your computer.

1. Switch on the NXT by pushing the orange button on the NXT.

2. Scroll to the Bluetooth icon on the NXT with the gray triangle button.

3. Push the orange button.

4. Scroll to "Visibility" and select "Visible" by pushing the orange button.

5. Scroll to "On/Off" and select "On" by pushing the orange button.

When you connect your computer to the NXT brick via your operating system, you will be prompted for a "passkey." The default is 1234. You can enter your own passkey if you want, but make sure you do so on both the computer and the NXT brick.

Once you have made the connection to the NXT via Bluetooth from the computer, the Controller in the NXT-G Software will allow you to select the connected NXT brick. If you have more than one, I recommend giving each a unique name to avoid confusion when making connections—you would hate to download programs to the wrong robot.

Note   Bluetooth communication is not allowed at some LEGO robotics events, such as FIRST LEGO League. So if you're used to using Bluetooth to download program updates, remember to bring a USB cable when you go to competitions.

If you are not using Bluetooth on your NXT brick, turn it OFF to save battery life. With Bluetooth ON, your NXT is using power trying to find systems to connect.

Firmware

Firmware is a very small program that is stored on your computer or, in this case, the MINDSTORMS NXT brick. It tells the NXT how to handle very low-level operations and how to use instructions from your NXT-G programs. Firmware is a program that you do not change; once you load it onto the NXT brick, it will remain there until you override it with a newer version.

Within the NXT-G software Tools menu there is an option for "Update NXT Firmware." The dialog box in Figure 1-13, will show you the current firmware versions loaded on your system and will allow you to check the LEGO MINDSTORMS website for any updates.

Figure 1-13. Firmware Dialog box

If you are programming your NXT for a robotics competition or similar event, avoid updating your firmware mid-season. Rarely will firmware upgrades cause issues with existing NXT-G programs, but there is no guarantee that you won't run into trouble from an upgrade. Therefore, I advise checking for an update at the beginning of the season and then sticking with that version of the firmware unless there is a known issue with the version you are using.

Note   You cannot do a firmware update via Bluetooth; you must use the USB cable connection.

Checking the LEGO MINDSTORMS website will alert you to any known issues with the current firmware versions available. In the Update Firmware Dialog box seen in Figure 1-13, the "Check" button will take you to the LEGO MINDSTORMS website and check for newer releases of the NXT firmware.

Summary

As you spend more time developing winning programs for your MINDSTORMS NXT robot, you will become more familiar with the NXT-G Software and its interface. This introduction only touches on some of the basic navigation; in the following chapters we will learn about more detailed functionality of many of the tools available to you in the NXT-G software.

Chapter 2

Software Design Process

Where to start? Before you can jump in and start creating your program, you have to spend some time figuring out what the program needs to do and how you plan to do it. This thought process, mapping out and thinking through the program logic is your design process. If you're working as a member of a team, you will have to do this process as a group, and it can be a challenge for team members to agree on the best way to do things. Remember to be open to all ideas during the design process. An idea that seems a bit crazy could actually be the best solution to the problem at hand.

Choosing the Right Problem

The first step in writing good code is to make sure you understand the problem you are trying to solve. If you are on a FIRST LEGO League (FLL) team, you will have a series of missions your team is trying to complete to gain points. It's a wise idea to sit down as a team and organize the tasks in order of difficulty,easier mission first and the harder missions last. Some teams might sort the missions by their value in points, but if you focus solely on the missions that give you the most points, you might find yourself spending way too much effort on a harder mission when you could have done some of the easier missions and scored more combined points.

FIRST LEGO LEAGUE (FLL)

The FLL is an international competition organized by FIRST for elementary- and middle-school students (ages 9–14 in the United States and Canada, 9–16 elsewhere). It is a joint effort through a partnership between FIRST and the LEGO Group.

Every year, a new robotics challenge is given to teams. These challenges are based on real-world scientific issues. Teams work on building LEGO MINDSTORMS robots to complete as many of the challenges as they can with in a given time frame.

If you look at the points-ordered list of missions in Figure 2-1, you see that "Bring the car to base" is worth the most points. But when you look at the list of missions ordered by difficulty in Figure 2-2, you notice that the "Bring the car to base" is the most difficult while the "Carry recycled parts to center" is easier, and if you're able to do all six items, you get a cumulative score of thirty points.

25 pts - Bring Car to base
15 pts - Empty barrels from bin
10 pts - Turn house window 90 degrees
8 pts - Deliver boxes to depot area
8 pts - Deliver minifigs to home
5 pts - Rotating windmill
5 pts - Carry recycled parts to center (6 items @ 5pts ea)
5 pts - Grab spinning top first

Figure 2-1. *List of missions in order of points*

Easy - Carry recycled parts to center (6 items @ 5pts ea)
Easy - Grab spinning top first
Med - Turn house window 90 degrees
Med - Deliver minifigs to home
Med - Rotating windmill
Hard - Bring Car to base
Hard - Empty barrels from bin
Hard - Deliver boxes to depot area

Figure 2-2. *List of missions in order of difficulty*

However your team decides to order the missions, it's important to have a road map of each mission you will attempt to complete with your robot. The goal is to design a program that cannot only solve a mission but that can do it consistently over and over. A program that can complete its mission every once in a while is not going to give you any awards; it will give you only headaches. Try not to get frustrated if the first solution you come up with doesn't work as expected. During the design phase of your programs, you will make multiple attempts at finding the desired solution.

What you're doing here is called Iterative design. This is a design methodology based on a circular process of designing, writing, testing, analyzing, and refining a program. Based on the results of testing the most recent iteration of a design, changes and refinements are made. This process is intended to ultimately improve the quality and functionality of a program.

Define the Problem

When starting, you need to fully understand the problem you are trying to solve. With FLL, the problem will be the mission you are trying to complete. Make sure you read and understand the game rules for each mission. Also, be aware of any changes to the rules before you attend your robot event. There is nothing worse than showing up to compete and finding out that you have been practicing with the wrong rules or that you have an improper understanding of the rules.

Many of the missions will have multiple steps involved, so break down the steps into simple-to-understand tasks. Don't try to write them as a program right now; just list the steps in simple-to-understand language. Act as if you were explaining the mission to friends and you want to tell them what needs to be done to complete the mission.

If you were to break down a mission that involved a robot grabbing an item and returning with it to your base area, the list might look something like Figure 2-3. The process of "breaking down" a mission involves reading the rules and understanding each task required by the robot to complete the mission. Even though some of the tasks may seem insignificant or obvious, you will need to include them in your list. Every little detail is important at this point.

Leave base
Find North wall of table
Grab spinning top
Return to base

Figure 2-3. *List of tasks for the "Grab spinning top" mission*

Having a simple list of tasks for a mission can make even the most complicated missions seem much less complicated. If any of your tasks are overly complex, you may need to break the task down even further. The goal is to keep things simple and easy to understand. For example, in Figure 2-4 you see a more complicated task list for a mission that involves locating a car on the game field and returning it to base.

Leave base
Follow wall to east wall
Find black line on field
Follow the line to the X
Grab the car
Back up to south wall
Return to base

Figure 2-4. *List of tasks for the "Bring car to base" mission*

In this list, you notice that one of the tasks is to "Grab the car." To you this may seem simple, the logic being that the robot will use a claw attachment to simply grasp the car. But once you write the code for the "simple" task, you will find that it's not as easy as you first imagined. The task of grabbing can involve some more complicated logic, such as:

- What state is the claw currently in? Is it opened or closed?

- Is it opened enough to fit the car?

- How do you close the claw attachment?

- When do you know that the claw actually has the car in its grasp?

Write Pseudo code

Once you have the list of tasks, it's time to think about how to make them work. You are still not ready to write NXT-G code. What you'll start with is called "pseudo code," which is writing out, in human-readable form, how to do the tasks. You will still list out the commands needed to complete the tasks—you don't need all the details that the computer cares about. Pseudo code is easier for people to understand than the NXT-G programming language. In Figure 2-5, the teammate's pseudo code is being presented to her team members. Being easy to understand is important when you need to explain your ideas to other teammates and the technical judges at your event.

Figure 2-5. Teammate Amy presenting her pseudo code to her team

Note   Saving your early design documents is a good idea. It's recommended that you keep all your design work in a notebook as you go along. This notebook can be helpful when you need to present your design logic to a panel of technical judges at your robotics event.

You can also use flow charts for more complicated solutions. If your tasks include lots of conditional logic, it helps to map out the possible paths the logic could take. A flow diagram can help you keep things in perspective and not get lost in the logic flow. Figure 2-6 is a sample flow diagram as presented to a team.

Figure 2-6. *Presenting flow diagram of logic*

Mapping your code out in these forms helps you find any possible flaws in the logic before it gets to the actual code stage. Also, it allows you to work with your team and share different ideas and receive input from others to improve the solution.

Identify Possible Solutions

When working with a large team, it can be hard for ideas or solutions to be heard from everyone. It's important to remember that teamwork is a big part of a successful team, and teamwork is judged in FLL. A good idea is to break into smaller groups (or even individuals) and work on your pseudo code to solve the current mission task.

Once everyone has his solution ready, come back as a group and present the solutions to the team. This is where having readable and easy-to-understand pseudo code comes in handy. Flow diagrams can be helpful as well, since they will give your teammates a visual idea of what you're thinking.

Now that the ideas are being presented, it's a good time to get input from other teammates. Don't take any new ideas or criticisms personally. You are all working toward the same goal—having a dependable and well-thought-out program that will solve the mission effectively and consistently.

Sharing ideas in a free-form manner is sometimes called a "brainstorming session." In such a session, there is no such thing as a bad idea. All ideas and solutions should be welcomed. This doesn't mean that they will work, or even be feasible, but by sharing these ideas, the group might form new ideas and solutions. Again, remember not to take suggestions or criticisms personally—there are no wrong answers or dumb ideas in brainstorming sessions.

Create the Code

Now that you have a possible solution, it's time to put it into action by creating real NXT-G code from your pseudo code. Once you get some experience with NXT-G, you'll find your pseudo code becoming closer to real code as you use command names that are similar to the block names used in NXT-G. This will make the transition easier and the creation process smoother.

For example, let's presume your pseudo code looks something like this:

1. Raise attachment arm up

2. Move forward 6 inches

3. Turn 90 degrees to the right

4. Back up 3 inches

5. Drop attachment arm down

The NXT-G blocks are very straightforward in this scenario. All of the tasks defined are "action" tasks, so most of the time they will involve using the Move or Motor blocks in NXT-G. Figure 2-7 shows some NXT-G code that might be generated based upon the preceding list of steps.

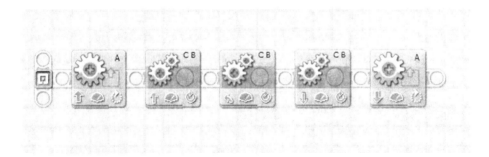

Figure 2-7. Simple NXT-G code created from pseudo code

Now look at a more complicated list of tasks, such as:

1. Move forward

2. Stop when Touch sensor on port 1 is bumped

3. Drop attachment arm

4. Turn 90 degrees to the right

5. Move forward

6. Stop when Light sensor on port 3 sees Black

7. Lift attachment arm

With this list of code tasks, you can see that there are some "action" tasks as well as some "sensor" tasks, which involve touch sensors and light sensors. The NXT-G code in Figure 2-8 is an example of what your final program might look like.

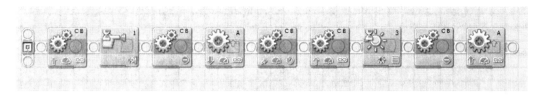

Figure 2-8. More complicated NXT-G code created from pseudo code

Let's look at an even trickier list of program tasks. This list involves "action", "sensor," and "conditional logic" tasks:

1. Move forward 3 inches

2. Turn 90 degrees right

3. Move forward

4. If Light sensor 1 sees a value greater than 50% turn right

5. If Light sensor 1 sees a value less than 50% turn left

6. When Ultrasonic sensor 1 detects object at 3" Stop

As you can see in Figure 2-9, the logic has grown more complicated and might be hard to read as NXT-G code. The code is easier to understand when you reference the preceding pseudo code.

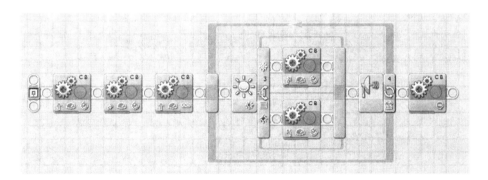

Figure 2-9. Simple NXT-G code created from pseudo code

It would be a good practice to include the pseudo code as comments in the NXT-G code; doing so will make it easier for you and team members to understand what the code is doing when you reference it later. Even though code that you write makes sense to you on the day you write it, in a week or so you may forget what the logic flow for the program was intended to be.

Test the Solution

When you run your new program on your robot, don't get upset if it does something you didn't expect. Rarely does the first attempt at any program work as you desire, and even the simplest solution might need some "tweaking" to get it just right. This is true for anyone who writes software programs of any type.

The best thing to do during testing is to run the new program multiple times and see if you get the same result each time. Even if it does what you expected, run it a few more times and see if the successful outcome repeats itself consistently.

If your program is not working as expected, observation is going to be your best tool in determining what is occurring with your program. Running a robot program over and over while making detailed observations is a very helpful debugging technique. A good trick is to, while the robot is running, verbally identify which NXT-G blocks it's running as the robot goes through the program. Follow along while looking at the code on your computer screen (or while looking at a printout of your code).

Often the first reaction is to blame the robot for the code not working correctly, as in thinking that the actual robot hardware is defective or malfunctioning. This is very rarely the situation. Remember, the robot is a computer, and computers are only as smart as the programs they run. They do exactly what they are told to do. So if something is not working as you expected, it's because you told the robot to do what it is doing and not necessarily what you wished for it to do. You might not have intended to tell the robot to do the wrong thing, but if you check your code carefully you will find that the robot is doing only what it was told.

Have other teammates look at your code as well. Often when we write code we have a hard time seeing the flaws in our own work. A second set of eyes might see a flaw in either the code or the logic itself that you missed.

In Chapter 4, we'll spend time talking about lots of helpful tools and tricks for debugging your code when simple observation isn't enough.

Summary

Working in a group to develop software can be challenging at first, but if you go into the process with an open mind, you will find that not only do you end up with better program ideas, you learn new ideas by seeing how others handle the same problems in different ways than you do. This kind of input can make you a well-rounded developer.

Remember, the key to good code is to keep it simple. This not only helps you and your teammates to understand how the code works, but it also leaves less room for error. What you want with code at a robot competition is code that works the same every time. Predictable and consistent results are a big part of a winning robot program.

Chapter **3**

Working with My Blocks

The NXT-G software comes with a large variety of useful blocks to help you build your programs, but it also includes the ability for you to create your own custom blocks, called "My Blocks." My Blocks contain collections of NXT-G software blocks that create subprograms or functions that you can reuse within other NXT-G software programs. The Common and Complete palettes contain the predefined NXT-G software blocks; the Custom palette is where My Blocks are accessed. In Figure 3-1, the blue block is the My Block that is included in the sequence.

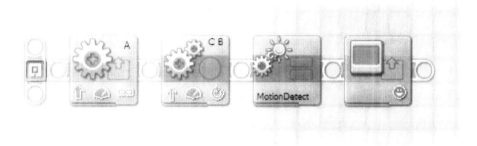

Figure 3-1. My Blocks are easy to spot in a sequence—they are colored blue

Why use My Blocks?

There are multiple reasons to make use of My Blocks in your programs. The first is the re-usability of common code. If you have a sequence of blocks that you find yourself using over and over in your programs, you can create a My Block that contains the common sequence. Then you simply add the My Block to your program whenever you need that particular sequence of blocks. Second, there is a limited amount of memory available on your LEGO MINDSTORMS NXT brick, so anything that helps you use less memory is helpful. Using My Blocks allows you to reuse code without requiring extra memory because the My Block uses only one location of memory no matter how many times you reference it. Last, My Blocks allow you to break up larger programs into smaller, more manageable pieces of code. When programs grow large, it can be hard to keep track of the logic, so when you group the different parts of logic into My Blocks, the code not only becomes easier to understand but it also can be much simpler to manage and debug. Even if you don't plan on reusing the My Blocks in other programs, they offer a good way to keep your large NXT-G programs organized.

Starting Off Simple

Let's work on creating a My Block called "DelaySequence" that plays a tone, displays an hourglass icon, and waits for four seconds. Creating this sequence will require only four NXT-G software blocks. The block can be used over and over to cause a program to pause for four seconds before continuing to process the program sequence.

To start out, put together an NXT-G program that includes the blocks that will be included in the DelaySequence My Block. In Figure 3-2, you can see the blocks that will make up the DelaySequence block highlighted in blue. Your program can contain other blocks as well, but only the highlighted blocks will be part of the new My Block.

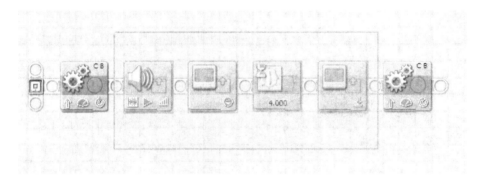

Figure 3-2. Highlighted blocks will make up the new My Block

Before the My Block is created, the code should be tested "as is" to confirm that it works as desired. It is much easier to test My Block code sequences when they're still in their native code sequence. In the code sequence, notice that the blocks highlighted are:

1. A Sound block to play an alert tone

2. A Display block that will show an hourglass on the NXT screen

3. A Wait block that will pause the program for four seconds

4. And finally, another Display block to clear the hourglass off display screen.

If you run the complete program seen in Figure 3-3, you will notice that the B and C motors run forward for five rotations, then wait for four seconds, and then run backward for five rotations. Once you are satisfied with how the program performs, you're ready to create the DelaySequence My Block.

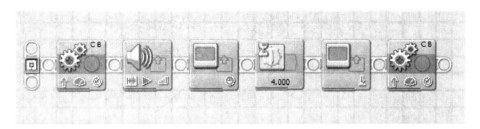

Figure 3-3. NXT-G code without a My Block

Start out by highlighting the blocks you want to include in the new My Block and then select the Create My Block button on the toolbar (Figure 3-4) or select "Make A New My Block" under the Edit menu item. The My Block Builder dialog box will launch with the four blocks you selected inside, as seen in Figure 3-5.

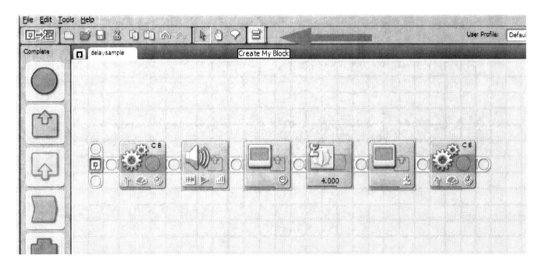

Figure 3-4. Selected blocks to make new My Block. Notice the cyan borders around the selected blocks

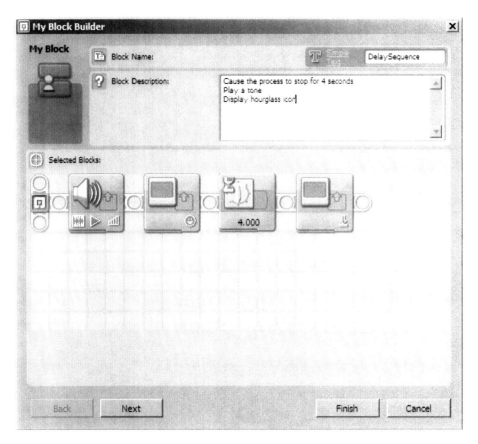

Figure 3-5. Create My Block Builder dialog

The highlights in Figure 3-4 are a tad difficult to see in black and white. You will see them on screen as cyan-colored borders surrounding each of the four blocks.

Try to give the block a name that describes its functionality to make it easier for others to know what the My Block does. We will name the new block DelaySequence. Don't make the name too long; even though the text box will allow long names, only the first 13 characters will be displayed on the My Block icon. The Description box gives you room to enter longer explanations of what the block does and how it will work.

When you select the "Next" button in the My Block Builder dialog, you will select an icon to represent your new My Block. If no icon is selected, the generic My Block icon will be used. On the icon-selection screen, you can pick any of the icons and drag them into the icon editor display. Multiple icon graphics can be selected and combined in the icon editor. Also, you can resize the icon image by selecting the little black squares that show up when you select the icon. In Figure 3-6, you can see that a custom icon has been created by adding the StopWatch, Music Note, and Play arrow icons.

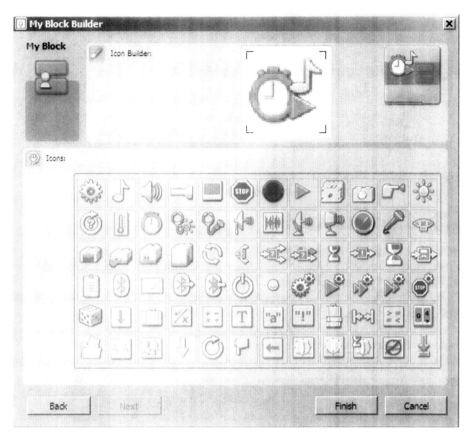

Figure 3-6. My Block icon builder

Press the "Finish" button and your new My Block, DelaySequence, has been created. Notice that your code now has the original four blocks replaced with the newly created My Block, as seen in Figure 3-7.

Figure 3-7. Code now including the new DelaySequence My Block

You may have some extra empty space on your sequence beam where the original blocks were located. By placing your cursor on the sequence beam and holding it down, you can drag the beam to the left to remove the empty space,as seen in Figure 3-8.

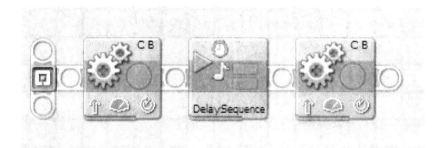

Figure 3-8. *Sequence tighten up with extra space removed*

Editing My Block contents

The blocks you used to create the new DelaySequence block are no longer visible in your program, but they are not gone. In order to view and edit the code inside of a My Block, simply double click on the block or highlight the block and select "Edit Selected My Block" from the Edit menu. This will cause a new tab to open on the workspace that will include the code sequence that is defined in the My Block. You will notice that the code tab has an icon with two blue bars that indicate that this tab represents code inside of a My Block versus a regular program. Figure 3-9 shows the DelaySequence My Block opened in the workspace.

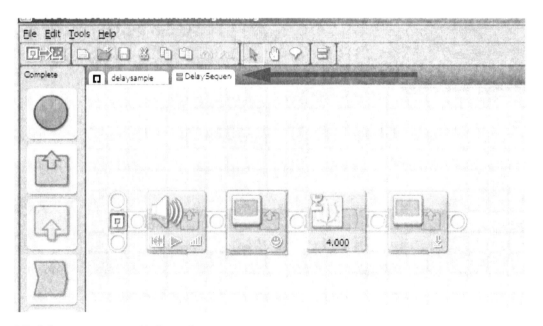

Figure 3-9. *Delay sequence opened in the workspace*

You can change the code blocks in the My Block workspace just as you do with any other NXT-G program. Remember, though, that any changes you make will affect all instances of the DelaySequence My Block, so be aware of everywhere you make use of this My Block and think of the consequences such use will have. This also has the advantage of the change being reused in other programs. For example, say you have a special My Block written for controlling the navigation of your robot by controlling the rotation of the motors. When you originally wrote this My Block, you were using 3-inch-diameter wheels. Now you change those wheels to ones with a 2.5-inch-diameter. By changing the necessary values in the navigation My Block, all of your programs that use the My Block will pick up this change next time they are compiled and reloaded to the NXT.

Note   All programs that use the My Block must be recompiled and loaded into the NXT for the change to be used by existing code.

You only had to change the code once, but it corrects the value in multiple programs. This can be very important at robot competitions, where you will have multiple programs being used on your robot for the day's event. It allows for quick changes with a minimum amount of work and risk.

MY BLOCK SAVES THE DAY

At one event, a team I was coaching realized that the placement of an Ultrasonic sensor on its robot was interfering with an attachment included on the robot. The team needed to move the Ultrasonic to a different location on the robot's chassis. By doing this, the distance values being used in its programs were going to be wrong because the sensor was now about an inch further back from the front of the robot chassis.

The nice thing was that the code used to read the Ultrasonic sensor's values was condensed into a single My Block and reused throughout the various programs the team was using. By changing the distance values in the My Block, the team could simply recompile all the programs that used this My Block and quickly get back on track with little risk or effort.

Using a My Block

Now that you have created this DelaySequence My Block, how do you take advantage of it in your programs? You will be able to use this new block just as you do any other blocks in the NXT-G software. If you go to the Custom palette, select the My Block palette, and expand I,t you will now see the new My Block you created (Figure 3-10).

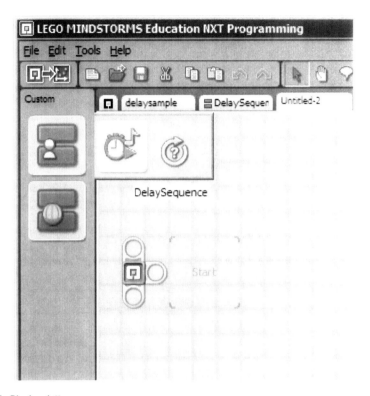

Figure 3-10. Custom My Block palette

To use it, simply drag the My Block to your sequence bar just as if it were a normal block. It can be added multiple times if you want to create more than one delay within your code, as in Figure 3-11.

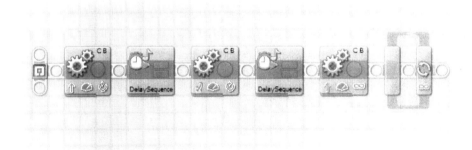

Figure 3-11. Code sequence using multiple My Blocks

My Block Properties

You will notice that many of the blocks that come with the NXT-G software have property values, or inputs, that show up in the Property panel when selected, as seen with the Motor block in Figure 3-12. Properties can be added to My Blocks as well to make them more flexible and useful in diverse situations.

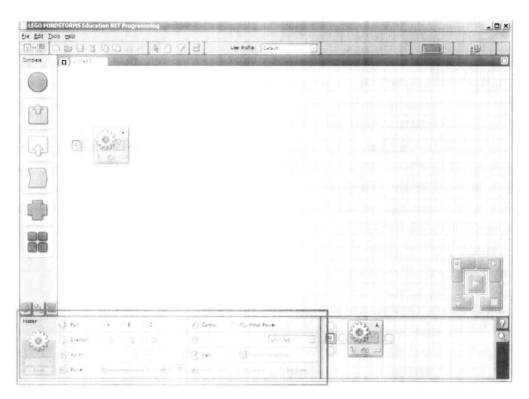

Figure 3-12. Motor block properties

Single Property

For example, say you have a My Block called TouchDown for lowering an attachment arm when the Touch sensor is pressed. Most of the time, the values in this block would not change. If you changed the design of the attachment arm, the rotation degrees needed to lower the arm correctly would possibly change.

In Figure 3-13, you can see the TouchDown My Block with hardcoded values for the number of degrees the Motor A will move to lower the attachment arm when the Touch sensor is pressed.

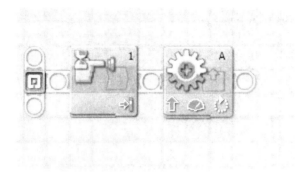

Figure 3-13. *TouchDown My Block with hardcoded duration value on the Motor block*

It would be nice to have a property value associated with the My Block to allow the value for the degrees moved to be adjusted. To do this, you will need to use Data Wires—this is how the NXT-G software transfers data between blocks, data such as numbers for power or speed values, logic values such as true and false and even text values that can be used for screen displays. Data Wires will be covered in more detail in Chapter 5.

In the case of the TouchDown My Block, the value for the Motor Rotate would need to be adjustable. First, we will have to start by recreating the My Block; property values cannot be added or removed after the My Block is created. This is a good reason to spend some time designing your My Blocks before creating them. Knowing ahead of time what properties your blocks will need can save you time spent to re-creating them every time you decide you need a new property.

In Figure 3-14, you can see the sequence of blocks used in the original TouchDown My Block, but there is a new block present as well. This is a Constant block. A Constant block holds a value, such as a number, logical (true or false), or text. In this example, it will be a number Constant that is connected to the Motor block's Duration property with a Data Wire. The idea is that whatever value is stored in the Constant will be the number of degrees that the Motor block is turned. The default will be 90 degrees, so the Constant block holds a numeric value of 90.

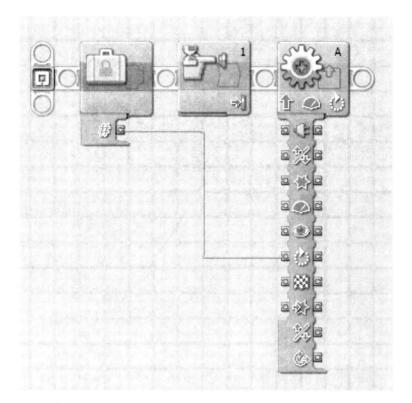

Figure 3-14. *Constant block wired to the Duration value of the Motor block*

To have the Duration value a property of the TouchDown My Block, you will highlight the original two blocks in the sequence that you had before leaving the new Constant block outside the selection. Since the selection will cross the Data Wire, the values outside the selection connected to the wires will become the properties of the new My Block. Highlight the desired blocks and select the Create My Block button on the tool bar as seen in Figure 3-15.

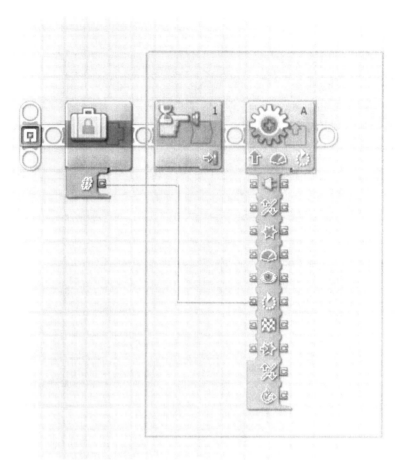

Figure 3-15. *New blocks selected for the TouchDown My Block. The Constant is left out of the selection*

In the My Block Builder dialog, you will notice that even though the Constant block is not part of the My Block definition, there is a Data Wire still that goes to a Data connector. This Data connector will become the property that is available on the newly created My Block. Step through the rest of the My Block Builder by naming the My Block TouchDown and select an appropriate icon for the My Block. Once the My Block has been created, you will see the new TouchDown block inserted into your program. There will be a Data Wire connecting the new My Block to the Constant block, as seen in Figure 3-16.

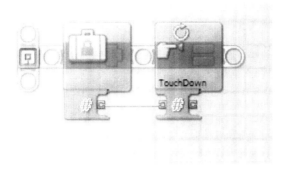

Figure 3-16. New TouchDown My Block connected to Constant block

When you select the TouchDown block, it now has a property associated with it. The property is currently labeled Duration, since that is where the Data Wire is connecting on the Motor block, as seen in Figure 3-17.

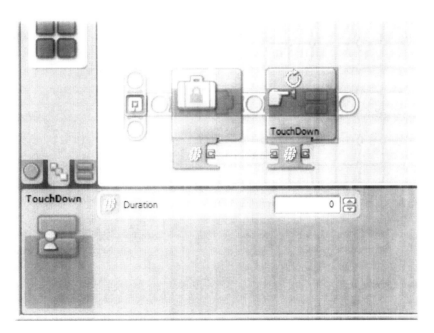

Figure 3-17. TouchDown My Block with the new property

If you want to change the name of the property, simply double click on the TouchDown block to edit the values. On the Data connector, you will notice the "Duration" label above the connector. If you cannot see the value, click on the Data connector and drag it so that you can see the label more clearly, as in Figure 3-18.

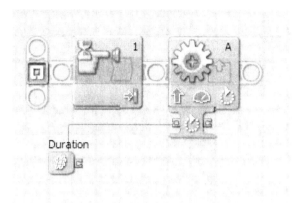

Figure 3-18. TouchDown block with property label

By highlighting just the label above the Data connector, you can change the value by typing whatever you wish for the property to be labeled as in your My Block definition. In Figure 3-19, the value is changed to "Arm Rotation Degrees."

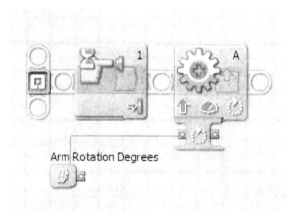

Figure 3-19. Property label renamed

When the TouchDown block is added to a program, it will now have the property Arm Rotation Degrees displayed in the property pane when selected, as in Figure 3-20. This property can be set either from the property pane or programmatically by using a Data Wire within your program's code.

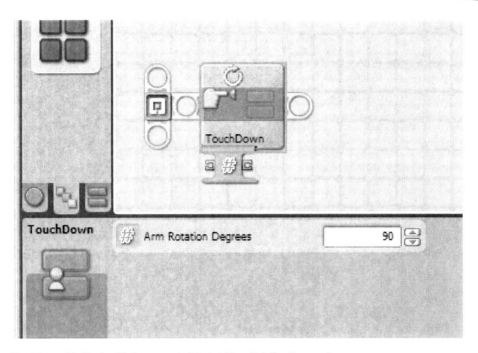

Figure 3-20. TouchDown My Block with the property labeled "Arm Rotation Degrees"

Multiple Properties

Often you will want to add more than just one property to a My Block, giving it more flexibility. Remember to plan the blocks out in advance, because once you add a property, it can be renamed but not removed or added.

Adding more than one property works the same as when you create a single property. You just need to make sure that your Data Wires are configured correctly so that when you make the selection of blocks to include in your new My Block that the Data Wires that represent the properties is located outside of the selection area.

As you can see in Figure 3-21, the code includes two Data Wires, one for the duration and one for the direction of the motor. The duration is connected to a numeric Constant block, and the direction is using a logic Constant block. But notice how the blocks are positioned on the sequence beam; there is no way to select the desired blocks (Wait Touch, and Motor) without including one of the Constants.

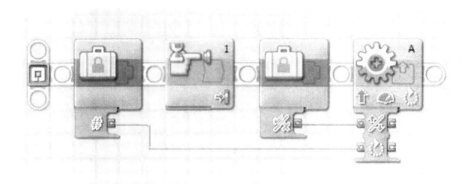

Figure 3-21. Block sequence to be used to create multiple-property My Block with Constants in wrong position

To fix this, you will need to reposition the Constants so that they are outside of the desired selection area, as seen in Figure 3-22.

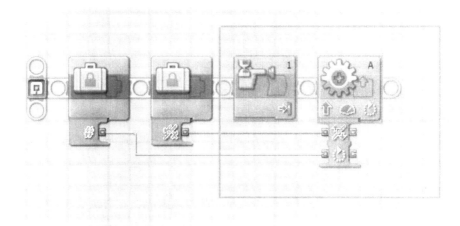

Figure 3-22. Block sequence with Constants outside of the desired selection area

Now you can select the desired blocks and create the new My Block. In the Create My Block dialog you will see the two Data Wires for your properties. Again you can double click on the labels an name the properties as desired.

Sharing Values

Another way to get data values into My Blocks is by using Variables. My Blocks maintain their own collection of Variables separate from the program that is using the My Block, but if you give a Variable the same name in your main program and the My Block, the Variable memory location will be shared between the two, thus allowing you to share values. So if you set the value of a Variable in your main code, it can be accessed by the code inside the My Block as well.

Managing and Sharing My Blocks

There will be times when you want to copy a block and reuse it. For example, the TouchDown My Block moves the Motor A so that it lowers the attachment arm on the robot when the touch sensor is pressed. What if you want a My Block that raises the attachment arm when the Touch sensor is released? That would use the very same blocks that are used in the TouchDown My Block but would just need a few minor changes. We can make a copy of the TouchDown My Block and create a new one called TouchUp.

To make the copy, select "Manage Custom Palette" from the Edit menu. A file dialog will open that shows you the contents of the My Blocks folder on your system. You will see the TouchDown My Block program listed. Just highlight it and select Copy from the Edit menu. Then select Paste from the Edit menu, and you will see a new file appear in the list. Highlight the new file and right-click on it (or press F2 on your keyboard) to rename the file TouchUp, as seen in Figures 3-23 and 3-24.

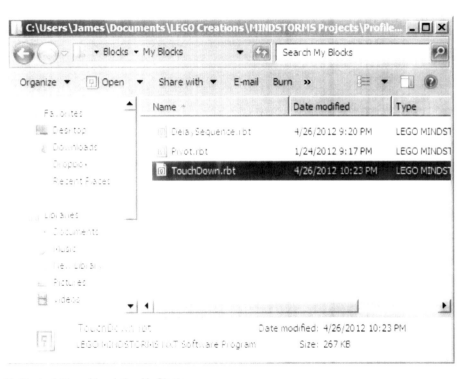

Figure 3-23. My Blocks folder with existing My Blocks

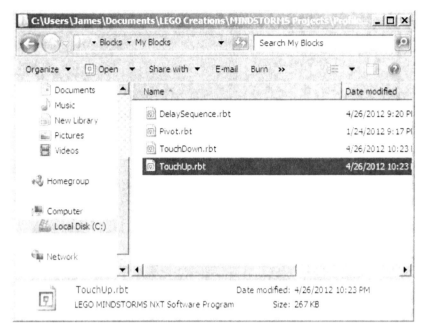

Figure 3-24. TouchDown block copied and named TouchUp

Now you can open the new TouchUp My Block so that you can change the code. When you first open it, you will notice that it has the same code as you had in the TouchDown program, as seen in Figure 3-25.

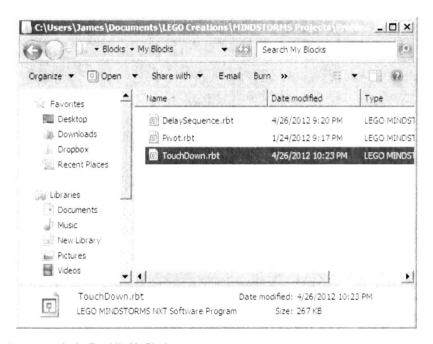

Figure 3-25. Block sequence in the TouchUp My Block

Change the Wait block to wait for the Touch sensor-release event and then change the direction on the Motor block. Once you make these changes, just save the program. You will now have a new TouchUp block on your My Blocks palette, as seen in Figure 3-26.

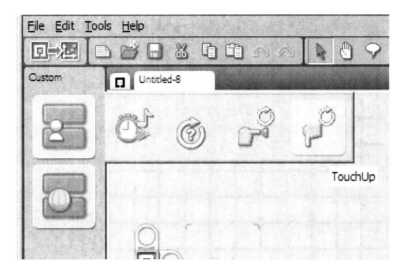

Figure 3-26. TouchUp My Block listed in the Custom My Blocks palette

You can also create a copy of a My Block by simply opening the code as you would for editing and then selecting the "Save As" option from the File menu. Be careful doing this, because anywhere the current My Block is referenced will update to use the new My Block name, and this may not be what you want.

Broken Blocks

When a My Block is being reference by a program, the My Block is not included in the actual program. It simply makes a reference to the My Block file. If this file is not present where the NXT-G software expects it to be, the My Block will be shown with a "crack" down the middle, as seen in Figure 3-27.

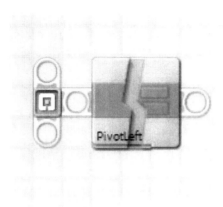

Figure 3-27. Broken My Block

This happens most often when a program is being shared between multiple computers. So when you copy the program from one machine to another, the My Blocks must be copied as well.

Pack and Go

NXT-G 2.0 has a tool that will help you transfer an NXT-G program between different computers. If you select "Create Pack and Go" from the Tools menu, you will be presented with the Create Pack and Go dialog box, seen in Figure 3-28. The dialog will show you a list of items associated with your program, such as the NXT-G program, My Blocks, and sound and image files. Give the Pack and Go package a name—make it something that reflects what the program does—then select OK. Now you have a nice package that you can give to someone else so she can load your program successfully onto her system.

Figure 3-28. Simple NXT-G code created from pseudo code

Summary

My Blocks can be a powerful tool in creating dependable and effective programs. They will give you the ability to better manage your code and to make changes quickly to your programs. Both of these points can be important at a robotics event.

With well-managed code, not only does it make it easier for you to understand, but it also will help the Technical judges understand. If a program is long and drawn out, the logic can be lost in the clutter, but if you break the code into logical My Blocks, everyone will understand what your program is doing.

Making changes quickly can be critical when you're under a short time frame at an event. Often a simple change to the robot design can create nightmares in your code if you must find everywhere you need to modify your code to reflect the hardware change. If your logic is broken into organized My Blocks, then, by making a few changes to the My Blocks, all of your code can be updated with little effort.

Chapter 4

When Things Go Wrong

Even the best-thought-out program can have unexpected issues. Some are easy to track down; others can drive you crazy trying to figure out what is going wrong. Again, you might be tempted to blame the robot as being faulty, but 99.99 percent of the time, that is not the case. The robot is doing exactly what it is told to do by your program.

Walking the Code

Sometimes just slowing down and "walking" through your code will help you find the solution. People tend to get upset or anxious about the program not working right, and then they have a hard time focusing. This is a good time to step back from the code and try to look at it from a different perspective—look at it as if you have never seen the code before. This may seem hard to do when you're at an event with time constraints, but rushing and being in a panic isn't going to fix the issue for you.

Look at each block in your code, talk out loud as a group about what the block is doing, and include the details. Things such as motor port assignments and sensor locations are important, so include them as you talk.

Doing a code walk through as a group can be helpful as well. During this process, find a whiteboard, large paper, or chalkboard someplace where you can write out the code and what logic is being executed. Writing it down as you go along can help you focus on what is happing in the program, and it can help you highlight any possible unexpected conditions.

Also, keep in mind the "state" of your values, sensors, and motors. The *state* refers to the current position or value. When doing your code walk-through, highlight the state of the different values with the logic flow.

It helps to bring in another team member who isn't as familiar with the code as you are, to look at the code with a fresh set of eyes. Often you are so close to the code that you miss the obvious problems that someone else could help you find. This is called a *Code Review* and is a process used in Software Engineering. Sometimes your solution to the problem might spring up when you talk to someone else, just because you are explaining your code.

Viewing Values

Being able to see the values that the program is evaluating can be very helpful, since you may be assuming that a particular value is something different than what the program is really seeing.

The NXT View menu

Built into the NXT firmware is the View submenu (Figure 4-1), which allows you to do a quick test of your data values from each of your sensors and motors. The values seen in the view menu are the values being returned at real time by the sensors and inputs on the NXT brick. The View menu is helpful in not only debugging values; it can also help when you're coding and need to know ranges of values to expect in your code.

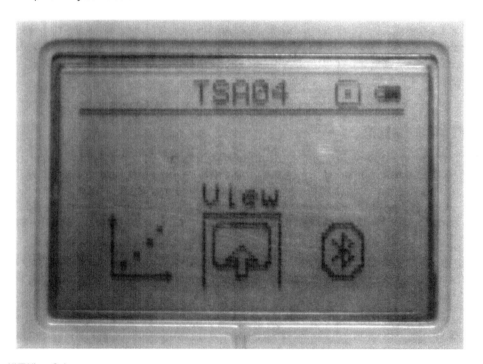

Figure 4-1. NXT View Submenu

To view the values of a sensor or motor, simply find the icon that corresponds to the type of sensor you wish to test. You can view only one sensor or motor at a time (Figure 4-2).

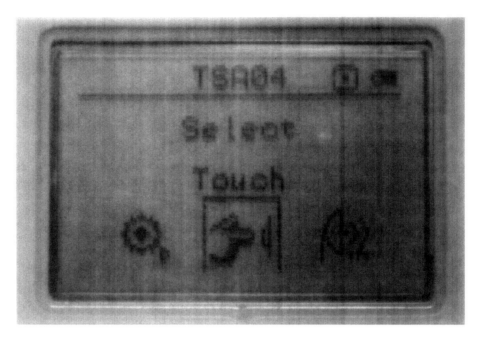

Figure 4-2. *NXT View Touch Sensor selection*

Next you need to select the port that the sensor or motor is using to connect to the NXT (Figure 4-3).

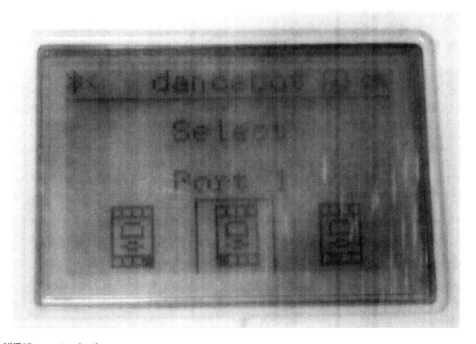

Figure 4-3. *NXT View port selection*

The data from the sensor will now appear on the screen (Figure 4-4). This is a good way to see different light sensor values or to check the rotation values coming from a motor.

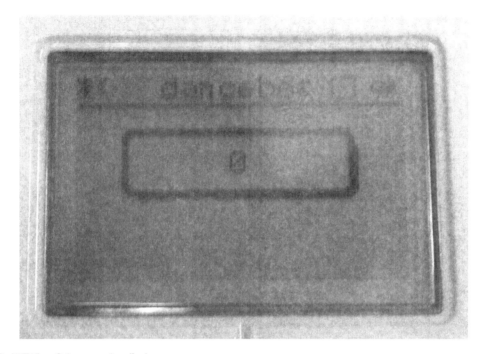

Figure 4-4. NXT View Submenu value display

My Block Viewers

The NXT View menu is helpful, but it doesn't always give you the help you need when trying to debug values in your program. For this, it's helpful to have some custom Debugging My Blocks handy. These blocks may seem simple and small, but having them condensed into a single My Block is very helpful.

The DisplayNumber My Block (Figure 4-5) is very helpful in displaying values of sensors while the program is running. Often you may anticipate a particular data value to be coming from a particular sensor but you find, by actually viewing the data while the program runs, that it is completely different from what you expected.

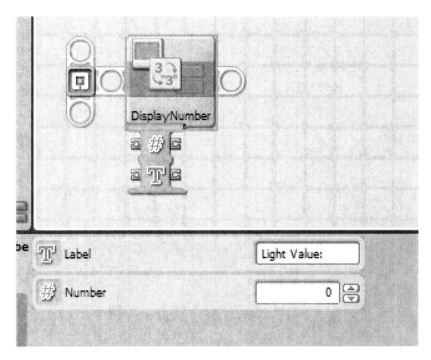

Figure 4-5. DisplayNumber My Block

In Figure 4-6, you can see the code that makes up the DisplayNumber My Block. Notice that it has two input values—one number and one text value. The text value will be a label for the value that is going to be displayed. For example, if you want to display the value of a light sensor, the label value would be something like "Light Value:".

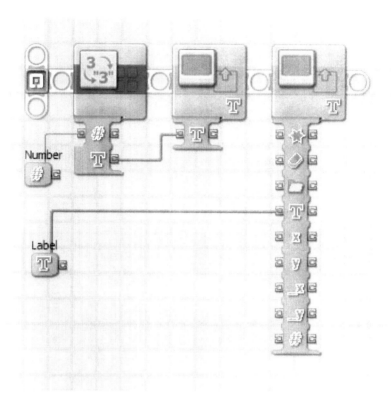

Figure 4-6. Code that makes up the DisplayNumber My Block

The number value is the numeric data coming from the particular sensor you wish to see. Sensors such as light and ultrasonic are good candidates for such values; the rotation of a motor would work as well.

Figure 4-7 shows the DisplayNumber My Block being used in a program to display the light value coming from a light sensor on Port 3.

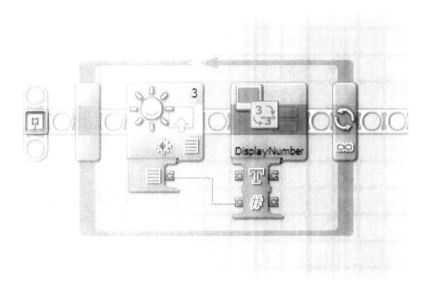

Figure 4-7. DisplayNumber My Block included in code

While the NXT View menu can only show only the value of one sensor at a time, the DisplayNumber My Block could be modified to include multiple values—for example, if your robot has two light sensors available and you want to compare the values at the same time. Figure 4-8 shows the DisplayNumber block modified to show multiple numeric values, and Figure 4-9 shows the block being used in code to display the values of the Light Sensors on Port 1 and Port 2.

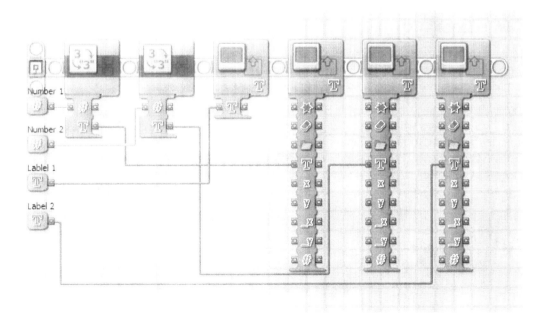

Figure 4-8. DisplayNumber My Block that allows for two numeric values

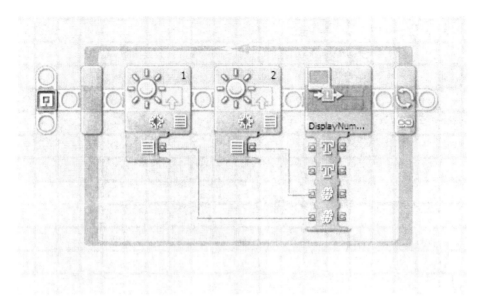

Figure 4-9. DisplayNumber My Block being used to display two Light sensor values

> **Note**   The light value you see with the NXT View menu is the uncalibrated value. To see the calibrated
> value, you need to use a block such as the DisplayNumber My Block. In Chapter 8, light-sensor
> calibration will be covered in detail.

Alert My Block

Visual clues, such as displaying of values, can be very important when debugging a program; audio
tones can be helpful as well. Often when your robot is running on the game field, you are not able to
see the display screen on the NXT, so having audio clues can be helpful.

By using a My Block such as the SoundTone in strategic locations within your code, you can use
your ears to understand where the robot is in the logic flow of the code. You can see the simple code
found inside the SoundTone My Block in Figure 4-10. Even though the SoundTone block contains
only a single sound block, having it in My Block allows you to reuse it without having to adjust a new
sound block each time.

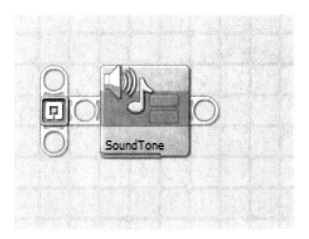

Figure 4-10. SoundTone My Block code

In the program shown in Figure 4-11, notice that the SoundTone My Block is used whenever the robot's light sensor passes a black line; the robot is supposed to stop at the third black line detected. Place the SoundTone My Block after the Wait block on the sequence bar to hear a tone each time the robot passes a line. Listen for the tones, and you can verify that the robot is recognizing lines as intended.

Figure 4-11. SoundTone My Block used in a line-detection program

The trick with counting black lines when you cross over them is that you have to read the beginning edge of the line as well as the ending edge to know that you have completely crossed the line. Once you have found both the beginning and the ending edge, you can add the line to your count.

In the same program, you could use both the SoundTone and the DisplayNumber block to add some extra help. The SoundTone would play at each line, but the DisplayNumber My Block could show the current count value on the NXT display screen, as seen in Figure 4-12.

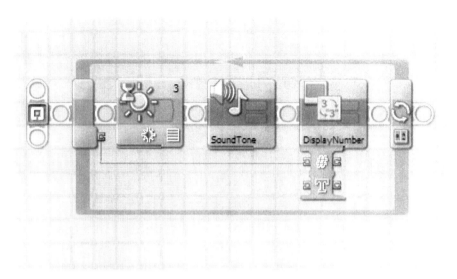

Figure 4-12. DisplayNumber block added to the code

Breaking the code down

Large programs can be very intimidating when you are trying to follow the flow and track down where things are not working as expected. As you learned in Chapter 3, My Blocks are a great way to contain code into logical sections.

If you look at the program in Figure 4-13, you will notice that it's a lot of code. Trying to follow and debug this program would be difficult.

Figure 4-13. Long NXT-G program

Now look at the same program broken up into logical My Blocks. The blocks are named in such a way that it's easy to know what each part of the program is supposed to do, making it self-documenting code. For example, there are blocks named: GrabBlocks, FollowLineToDropSpot, Pivot90, and DropBlocks (Figure 4-14). Even though none of these My Blocks will be reused, it still is a great use of My Blocks.

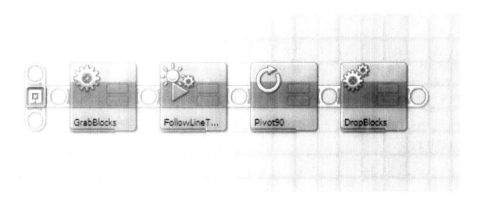

Figure 4-14. Code broken up into My Blocks

With the code broken into the smaller My Blocks, you can now test each part of the program separate from the others. Each My Block can be run as an individual program, allowing you to better isolate the logic and track down where things are not performing as you desire.

Common Mistakes

Often you may find yourself stuck when trying to find out why your code is not acting as you expect. There are some common conditions in NXT-G that can trip up a team. It's always a good idea to review these items when debugging a program.

Rotation Completion

Your program may seem as if it has come to a stop, while in reality it's still running, waiting for a particular task to complete. One common instance of this happening is when a Move or Motor block has been set for a particular distance. Say you have a Move block that is supposed to rotate a motor for 90 degrees, but something is blocking it from making a full motion. The blocking object could be the robot chassis or something on the field. Either way, the motor is only able to rotate, say, 80 degrees before becoming blocked. In this case, the NXT-G program will not continue on to the next block until the Move block is completed, and the Move block cannot complete because it still needs to rotate the motor another 10 degrees.

When you visually watch the robot run the program, it may appear that the robot has come to this Move block and just stopped working, while in truth it's waiting to complete the block. Check for these kinds of conditions if you feel your program has stopped unexpectedly. You may need to adjust the Move block's rotation distance or remove what is blocking the motor from completing its rotation.

Port Settings

One of the simplest things that catches people off guard when debugging is having incorrect port numbers set on their blocks. Often a team will be positive that its light sensor is connected to Port 1, but later, after much review, it will find that in fact, the light sensor is connected to Port 3. When multiple team members are working on a robot, it's easy for a wire to get reconnected to a different port. No matter how sure you are of a sensor's port connection, double check it.

Duration Value

Another common oversight can be the duration values set for Move or Motor blocks. If a robot is going too far, make sure that the duration is not set to Unlimited. Or, if the robot is not moving as far as you expected, check rotations versus degrees as the unit settings on the duration. It's easy to overlook these settings when using the Move and Motor blocks.

Environment

Another thing to take into account is the actual environment in which the robot is performing. Keep an eye out for layout or environmental factors that may make your robot work fine at your home practice field but then act differently at the completion site.

> **Note**   Lighting differences can play a big part in how the program responds. In Chapter 8, you will learn how to calibrate your light sensors to handle changes in lighting between venues.

Changing the light conditions in your practice area can be a good test to help avoid issues when you arrive at a competition event. Run the robot in the dark (or with very low room lighting). Then introduce some natural sunlight onto the game field. Many robot events are held in rooms such as school cafeterias which have lots of windows that allow natural sunlight to hit the tables. This can cause dark shadows that may affect your robot's program, or rather the program's interpretation of what the light sensor is "seeing" as the robot moves about the field. You can even go so far as to bring in different types of lights, such as shop lights, or shine flashlights onto the field, all to vary the lighting values on the game field to see whether that variation has any effect on your robot's performance.

Also look at things such as the field conditions; you may have a nice smooth field mat on your practice table but find that the mats at the competition are rippled or not aligned the same as yours against the two-by-four edges of the playing field. With proper programing, your robot should be able to adjust for these differences. Often the use of sensors to help a robot determine where it is on the field can help avoid issues associated with using just the rotation sensor as a navigation tool. You could test for field condition problems by adding some irregularities to your game field map. You can purposely put some wrinkles in the mat, or just shift it a bit out of being square with the table. If your robot's program can adjust for such issues, you will be better prepared for the unexpected in a competition event.

Summary

When your code is not acting as desired, the best approach is to try to think how the robot is "thinking." Analyze the logic and the values that are being presented to the program. Many times if you simplify things and get an understanding of the values coming into your program, you'll quickly find what is causing the issues.

Also take into account physical and environmental factors. When your robot is acting differently than it did at your practice location, take the time to survey the field and the location to see if you can identify anything that is different from what you're used to practicing with. Check the lighting. Check the alignment of the mat. Check for wrinkles. Look for physical factors that might affect your robot's operation.

Chapter 5

Moving Data

Many times, you will want your NXT-G program to remember various values and conditions. These values are stored as data in your NXT and can be shared within your programs among the different blocks. This data can be intimidating to transfer, but with some practice, you will find that it's not as difficult as it may seem.

Data Wires

Data wires give you the ability to transfer data between program blocks programmatically. You have seen that most blocks have a set of parameters that you can set or modify in the Properties panel. With data wires, however, you can access and change these values while the program is running (based on factors such as sensor readings or calculations). Many new programmers find data wires intimidating when first learning to program NXT-G programs, but by mastering the use of the data wires, you will find that your programs can become much more robust and effective.

Data wires send information from one data plug to another. Data plugs are located on the data hub of a block. When you click the bottom left of a block, the data hub will open to reveal the available data plugs used by that block, as seen in Figure 5-1. This is a toggle method, so clicking again will hide the block's data hub. Figure 5-2, from the NXT-G Help file, shows how each different data type is represented as a data wire.

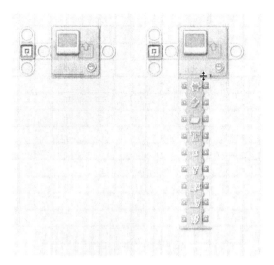

Figure 5-1. Expansion of the Display block's data hubs

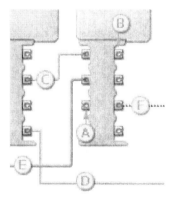

Figure 5-2. (A) Input data plug, (B) Output data plug, (C) Number (yellow), (D) Logic (green), (E) Text (orange), (F) Broken (gray)

For each property of a block, there will most likely be a data plug to represent it on the block's data hub. If a value has been entered for a block in the Properties panel, the data wire value will override that value.

Data wires can carry three different data types: Number (yellow), Text (orange), and Logic (green). If a wire is broken or connected to an improper data type, the wire will be displayed as a dotted gray wire.

By simply clicking a "broken" data wire, the Help panel reveals the issue that is causing the wire to be reported as improper, as seen in Figure 5-3.

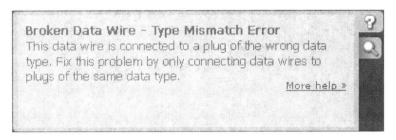

Figure 5-3. A broken data-wire message in the Help panel

To connect a wire, simply click the output data plug of the desired value. The cursor will change to look like a small spool of string (see Figure 5-4).

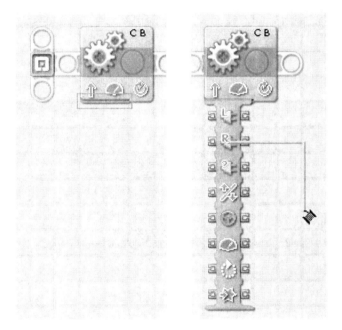

Figure 5-4. Data wire "spool" icon when dragging off a data hub

Now drag the wire to the input data hub of where you wish to connect the data wire. The data wires may seem a bit cluttered at first, but by simply closing and reopening a data hub, the autoalignment feature in the NXT-G will route the data wires so that they are more readable.

> **Tip** If you just drag the destination to the source (or vice versa), the NXT-G will reformat the data
> wires around the other blocks for you. Don't be surprised if the data wire comes from somewhere other
> than where you started it. If the data is shared among different blocks, the data wire may be rerouted
> from the shared block instead of the original block you chose.

Data wires can be removed simply by clicking them and pressing the Delete key. Also, when a block that has data wires connected to it is removed, the wires are removed as well. If you click the destination data plug, the connected wire is deleted as well.

As more advanced topics are covered in the following chapters, you will see the important role that data wires play in these programs.

Variables

Often in your programs, you will need to store a value of some type. The Variable block will allow you to do this; it gives you the ability to store a value to be used later in your program. Variables are commonly used for counters with number values for keeping track of whether things are on or off by using logic values.

The program in Figure 5-5 shows a simple program that will count the number of times a Touch sensor is pressed. The count value is stored in a Variable block called BtnCount. The steps for creating this program are explained in the section to follow.

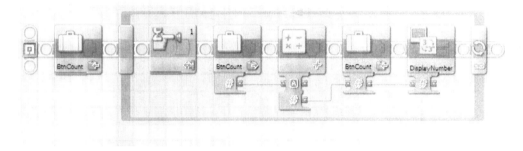

Figure 5-5. A simple program that counts the number of times the Touch sensor was pressed

How It Works

Think of the Variable block as a storage box, or as the icons in Figure 5-5 show, a little suitcase to hold your data values until you need to access them again. You can simply store the data by "writing" a value into the Variable block, and then later you can retrieve it by "reading" it so that you can evaluate the data.

Managing the Variables

Before you can make use of the Variable block, you will have to define the variables that will be used in your program. Selecting "Define Variables" from the Edit menu opens the Edit Variables dialog box (see Figure 5-6).

Figure 5-6. *Edit Variables dialog box*

You will have the ability to create new variables, name them, and define the data type that the variable will use. For example, to create a new variable for storing a counter of the number of times a Touch sensor was pressed, you start at the Edit Variables dialog box and then select the Create button. A new variable name will appear in the list of variables, as seen in Figure 5-7.

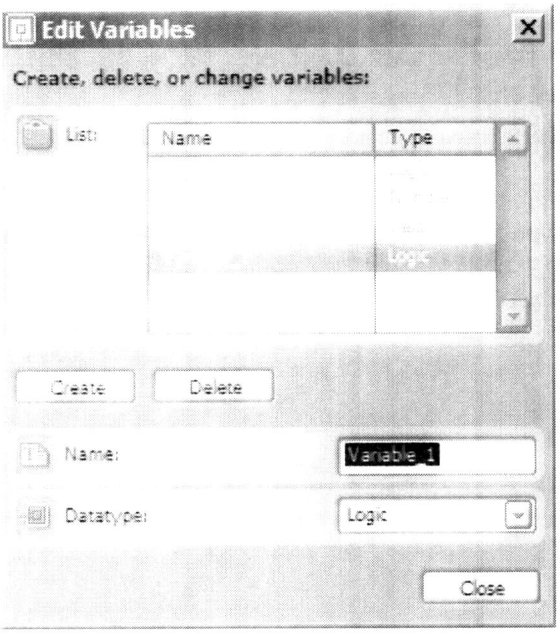

Figure 5-7. *Creating a new variable*

You can now give the variable a name and define the type of data that will be stored in this variable. There are three data types to choose from: Logic, Number, and Text (see Figure 5-8).

Figure 5-8. Variable data types

> **Note**   When naming a variable, select a name that makes it clear what kind of data the variable is going to store. Also keep in mind the length of your name: if it's too long, it will be truncated and unreadable on the Variable block.

Besides being able to create new variables, the Edit Variables dialog box allows you to change an existing variable name or type. If you change the name, it is changed everywhere the variable is used in your program. The same thing is true for the data type. Be careful, however, because if you have a Variable block wired to another block, and then change the data type of the variable, the wire will become broken and cause your program to not compile (see Figure 5-9).

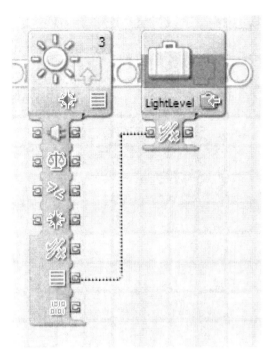

Figure 5-9. *Broken wire after data type change*

You can also delete a variable with the Edit Variables dialog box. If you try to delete a variable that is currently being used by a Variable block in your code, a warning message will appear, as shown in Figure 5-10.

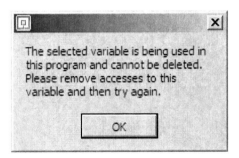

Figure 5-10. *Variable-in-use warning message*

Using the Variable Block

Once you have a variable defined, you can reference it with the Variable block that is found on

the Advance palette it looks like a little suitcase. When you add the Variable block to your sequence beam, the drop-down box lets you select the variable that will be used by the block. Also, the Variable block has two actions to choose from: Read or Write (see Figure 5-11).

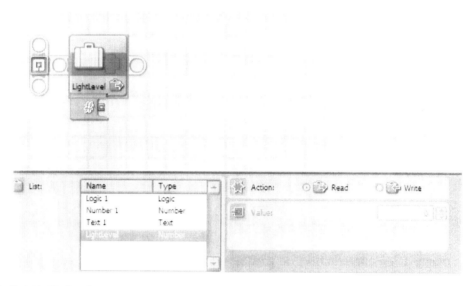

Figure 5-11. Variable block actions

In the next example, you will create a simple program that uses a number variable called Counter, which will keep track of the number of times the Touch sensor was pressed and display that value on the NXT screen.

Start a new program and call it **Counter**. Next, open the Edit Variable dialog box and create the new variable. Select the Create button and enter **BtnCount** as the variable and **Number** as the data type (see Figure 5-12).

Figure 5-12. *The Edit Variables dialog box for creating a new variable*

From the Data palette, add a Variable block that uses the new BtnCount variable to the beginning of your sequence beam. Set the action to "Write" and the value to 0. It is assumed that any new variable is set to 0 already, but it is a safe practice to initialize the value at the beginning of your programs. This ensures the values start out as expected (see Figure 5-13).

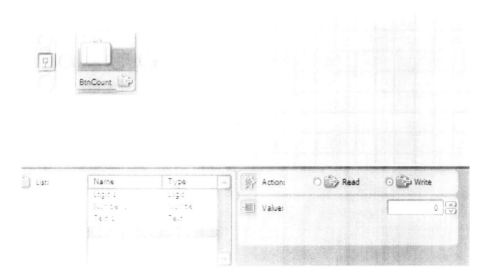

Figure 5-13. *Initializing the variable value at the start of the sequence*

Next, add a Loop block next in the sequence beam. Inside the loop, add a Wait block with the control set to "Sensor," the sensor set to "Touch Sensor," and the action set to "Bumped," as seen in Figure 5-14.

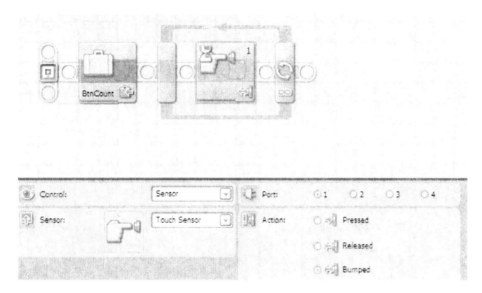

Figure 5-14. *Touch sensor Wait inside the Loop*

After the Wait block, add another Variable block that uses the BtnCount variable and the action set to "Read." Follow that with a Math block found on the Data palette. The operation is set to "Addition" and the B value is set to 1 (see Figure 5-15).

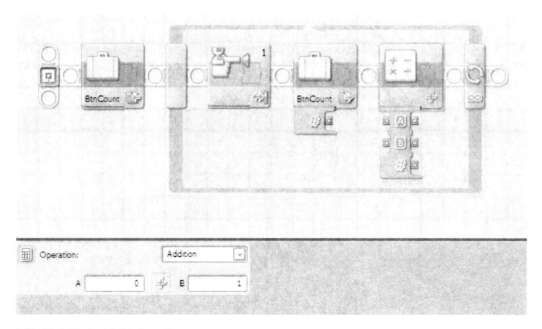

Figure 5-15. *Math block added to the code*

Include another copy of the Variable block, again set to the BtnCount variable and the action set to "Write." Wire the number output from the Variable block into the A input of the Math block, and then the number output of the Math block into the preceding Variable block. You are bringing in the current value of the BtnCount to the Math block, adding 1 to it, and then writing that new value back into the variable each time the Touch sensor is pressed and released (see Figure 5-16).

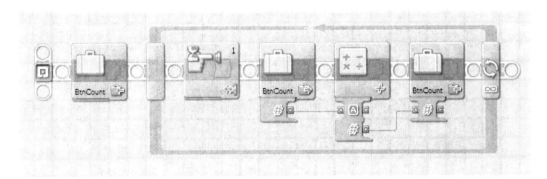

Figure 5-16. Touch counter code sequence

If you add the DisplayNumber My Block that was created in the previous chapter, you can see the value that is stored in the BtnCount variable, as see in Figure 5-17. When this program is run, it will now display the number of times the Touch sensor has been pressed on the NXT screen. You could even add a Sound block if you want a tone to play each time.

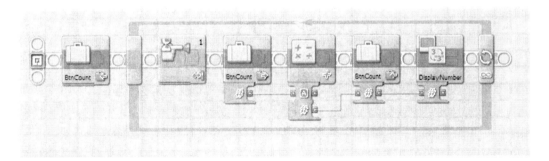

Figure 5-17. DisplayNumber My Block added to the sample program

This program might not seem very useful as it is, but think about it in a bigger program, like one in which your robot needs to keep track of the number of times it has bumped into a wall or items on the game field. Or instead of a Touch sensor, it could be counting the number of times it sees a certain color with the Light sensor. The idea is that by using the Variable block, your robot can keep track of certain data, thus allowing it to make smart decisions based on things it has learned and observed from its environment. A robot that can learn as it performs a task can be very helpful in events such as FLL.

Scope

The *scope* of data refers to the context within a program in which data is valid and can be used. Most of the time, a variable definition is local to your current program, but if your program includes a My Block that contains a variable with the same name in the main program, it will be treated as the same variable, thus allowing the value to be shared among multiple programs.

If you make a My Block out of the incrementing part of our recent Counter program, for example, the BtnCount variable will be shared between the two programs. Remove the wire between the last Variable block and the DisplayNumber My Block, and select the three blocks that make up the actual counting of the program, as seen in Figure 5-18.

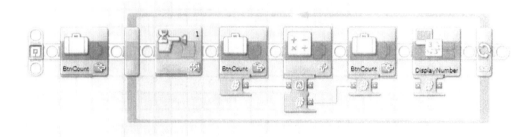

Figure 5-18. Select the counting logic

Create a My Block called **Increment**. Your code should now look like Figure 5-19.

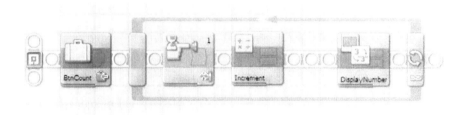

Figure 5-19. New Increment My Block

Add a Variable block that uses the BtnCount variable after the newly created Increment block, and connect the output to the DisplayNumber block (see Figure 5-20).

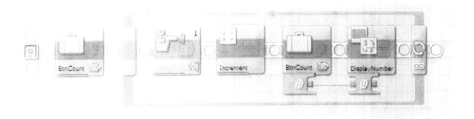

Figure 5-20. Wiring up the Increment My Block

If you run the program, you will see that you get the same results as you did prior to the My Block being added. This means that the BtnCount variable has global scope to the program. By opening the Increment My Block, you can see the BtnCount variable in place (see Figure 5-21).

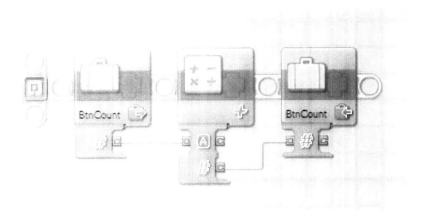

Figure 5-21. Increment My Block code

Constants

There are times when the values of your variables don't change. If you use variables for settings, these values will most likely remain consistent throughout the running of your program. Variables that don't change values are called *constants*. NXT-G 2.0 supports constants with the addition of the Constant block, which works similar to a Variable block but it doesn't have a "write" action, only the ability to be "read."

An interesting thing about constants in NXT-G is that when you define a new constant in the Edit Constants dialog box, the constant is available for any programs created on that computer. This is similar to My Blocks. For example, you have a constant called "WheelInch" that defines the number of rotations needed to turn your robot's wheels one inch forward. Every program that you write for your robot can reuse this constant when you need to move the robot forward a particular distance. If you decide to change the wheel size on your robot, the WheelInch value will need to change to hold the corrected number of degrees to move the robot forward an inch. The great thing is that if you change the defined value, the value will be changed in all the programs that reference this constant—and you don't have to search through all your programs to make the change in various places.

> **Note**   For the value of a changed constant to be recognized, you have to open the referencing program and resave it. Also, unlike a variable, if you change the name of an existing constant, the name change will not be reflected by any program that references that constant.

Defining a Constant

To write a sample program that makes use of a constant, start by creating a new program. From the Edit menu, select Define Constants. This will cause the Edit Constants dialog box to appear.

Just as in the Edit Variables dialog box, you will have a list of defined constants and Create, Edit, and Delete buttons. Select the Create button, and then input **WheelInch** as the Name, **Number** as the data type, and **2.6** as the value. The dialog box should look like Figure 5-22.

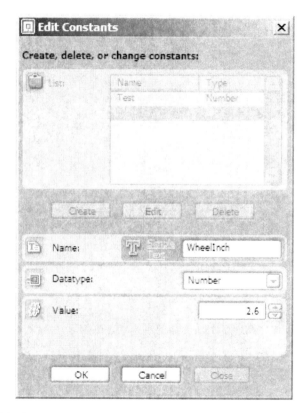

Figure 5-22. Edit Constants dialog box

Now add a Constant block from the Data palette. It will look like a suitcase with a padlock on it. In the Constant block properties, set the action to "Choose from list" and select the WheelInch constant in the list (see Figure 5-23).

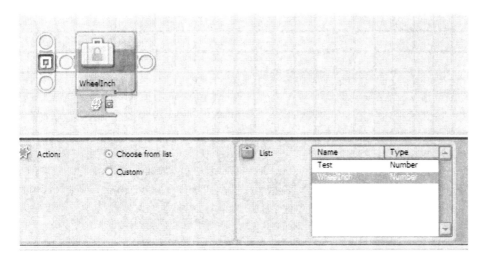

Figure 5-23. Constant block icon

Add a Math block afterward, followed by a Move block. The Math block should have its operation set to "Multiplication" and the B value set to 3. Wire the number output of the Constant block to the A input of the Math block, and then the number output of the Math block to the Duration property of the Move block. Figure 5-24 shows how things look when done.

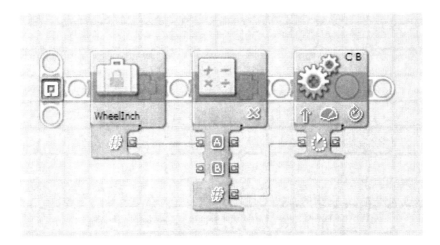

Figure 5-24. Sample program to move forward three inches

If you follow the logic of this code, it will take the value saved in the 2.6 constant (the number of rotations needed to move the robot one inch), then multiply it by 3, and pass that value to the Move block. This will make the robot move forward three inches. Later, if the diameter of the robot's wheels is changed, you only have to change the value of the WheelInch constant to match the number of rotations needed to move one inch. Recompile this program. The robot should move forward by the desired distance without any code having to be changed.

Custom Constant

The Constant block properties have two actions: "Choose from list" and "Custom". The Custom action allows you to define a constant locally within your program. When the custom action is selected, the properties of the Constant block will allow you to define the name, type, and value of the constant without having to use the Edit Constants dialog box. Be aware that constants defined this way are not available to other programs; the definition stays local within your program.

> **Note**   In the Edit Constants dialog box, if you create a new constant that has the same name as one defined with the custom action in a Constant block, the newly defined constant will override the value in the custom-action Constant block.

Also, if you delete a defined constant from the Edit Constants dialog box, any references to that constant will be replaced with a custom-action Constant block. Or if you transfer an NXT-G program from one computer to another, and the definition for a constant is not present on the new computer, it will be converted to a custom-action Constant block as well.

For example, let's say Laura has a program that she has written on her computer and she gives the program to Lee. If Laura's program has a Constant block that references a constant called LightLimit, but Lee's computer does not contain the same definition, the Constant block will be converted to a custom action instead of a reference to the constant. The values, type, and name will remain the same however (see Figures 5-25 and 5-26).

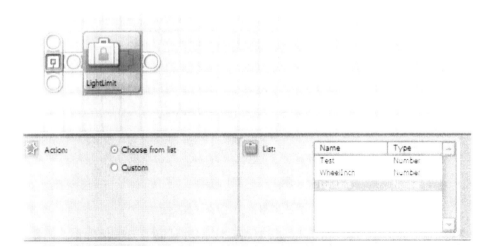

Figure 5-25. Constant block with defined constant

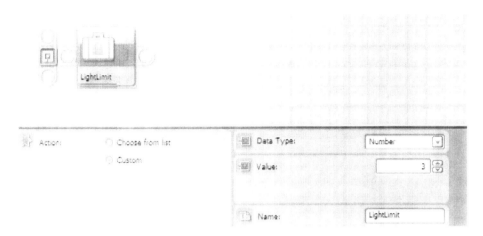

Figure 5-26. Constant block with custom action

Summary

Giving your program the ability to adjust and think for itself is critical to making a smart and winning program. Transferring and saving data throughout the program is the first step in writing "smarter" programs for your robots.

In future chapters, this concept will help your robot's program investigate and adapt to its environment, giving it an edge over programs that contain hard-coded values and that do not have the flexibility to think for themselves.

Chapter 6

Making Smart Decisions

NXT-G gives you the ability to program a robot that can evaluate conditions and values that are presented to it. It allows your robot to make choices based on these values; whether it makes smart choices is up to you. Using the tools that are available, you can program your robot to better navigate and solve tasks by "thinking" for itself instead of being hard-coded in what it will do when it hits the game field. Smart robots are winning robots.

Switch Block

The Switch block is found on the Flow palette and by default is set to evaluate the values of a Touch sensor, but it can be used for much more complex evaluations as well, including values of variables. Figure 6-1 shows the Switch block in its default state.

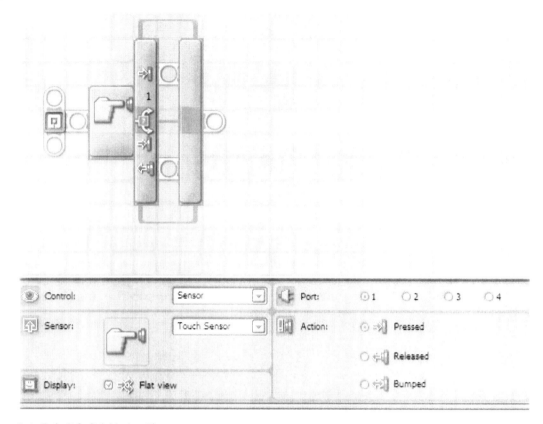

Figure 6-1. Default Switch block settings

You can see that the Switch block contains a pair of sequence beams; one beam is followed if the condition is "true" and the other beam is followed if the condition is evaluated as "false." You can add program blocks on these beams, and they will be run based on the state of the Switch block.

> **Note**   A Switch block is a simple State machine. A *State machine* is a device that stores the status of a value and can run an event based on a change to that value. Some State machines are simple and have only values of True or False, while others can have a larger set of possible values.

Basics

A basic example of the Switch block would be a program that plays a tone and displays a smiley face on the NXT when the Touch sensor on port 1 is pressed. To start, move a Switch block to the sequence beam, as seen in Figure 6-2.

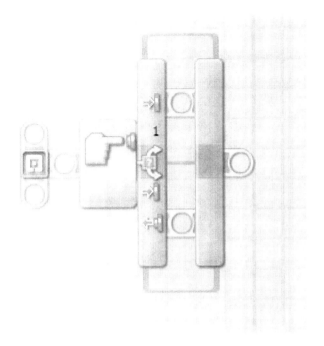

Figure 6-2. Switch block added to sequence beam

You will notice that the default settings for the Switch block are already configured for a Touch sensor on port 1. The upper sequence beam in the Switch block will run when the Touch sensor is pressed (or True) and the lower sequence beam will run when the Switch block is in its default state of being unpressed (or False). If True, you want to play a tone and display a smiley face, so add a Sound block and a Display block to the upper sequence beam. On the lower sequence beam, simply add a Display block to clear the display when the button is not pressed. Include this logic inside a forever loop so the condition of the Touch sensor can be checked repeatedly (see Figure 6-3). These are also referred to as "switch loops," and are used throughout programs to help control program flow.

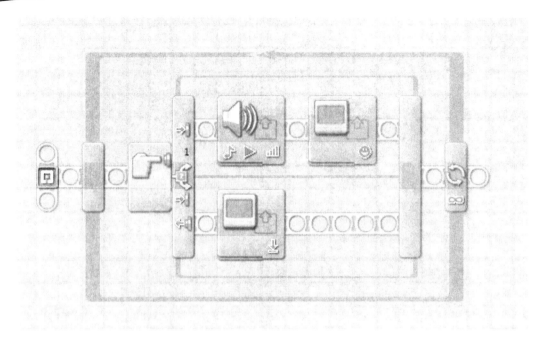

Figure 6-3. Loop block surrounding Switch block logic

Is the Touch sensor pressed? Yes or no? This is the logic being presented to the Switch block. If you were drawing a flow diagram, it would look something like Figure 6-4.

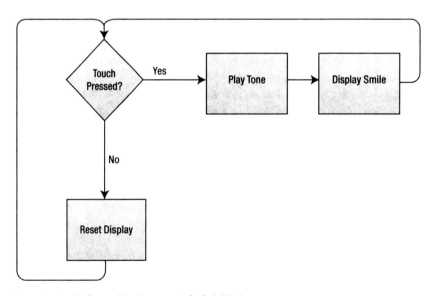

Figure 6-4. Flow chart showing logic used by the sample Switch block program

The previous example showed how to deal with simple on or off (pressed or not pressed) states, but you can also evaluate numeric values or ranges. For example, you can test whether a value is greater than or less than a given input value.

In Figure 6-5, you can see a program that is evaluating a raw numeric value coming in from a Light sensor and playing one of two different sound tones based whether the value is higher or lower than 50.

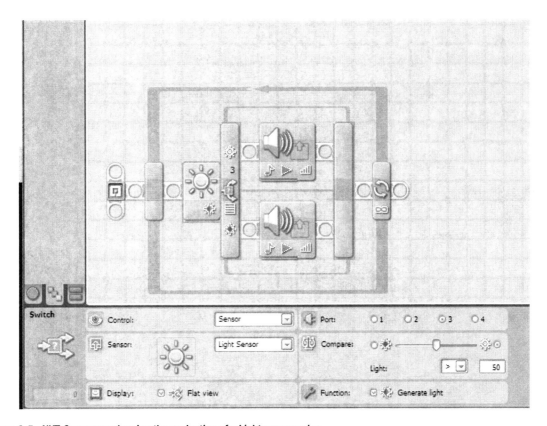

Figure 6-5. NXT-G program showing the evaluation of a Light sensor value

Advanced Switching

A simple Yes/No switch is easy to follow, but many times the decisions are a bit more complicated and require more than two options. On the Switch block, there is a property called Display. The default "Flat view" value is checked. If you uncheck this property, the Switch block will change and you will no longer see the pair of sequence bars but instead a series of tabs across the top of the block, as seen in Figure 6-6.

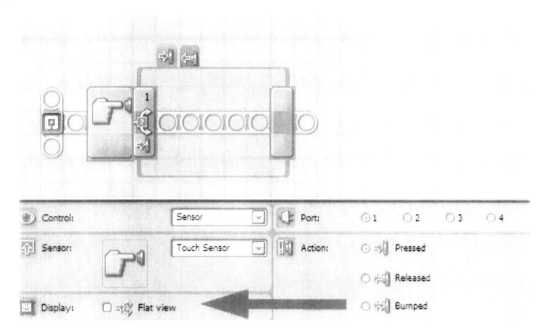

Figure 6-6. Tabbed view Switch block with Flat view unchecked

Now since the Touch sensor only has two states, pressed or not pressed, there are only two tabs. If you use the same sample program described earlier, and uncheck the Display property, you will notice as you click between the two tables that the blocks on the sequence bar will toggle between the values that were set up when Flat view was enabled. Figures 6-7 and 6-8 show this.

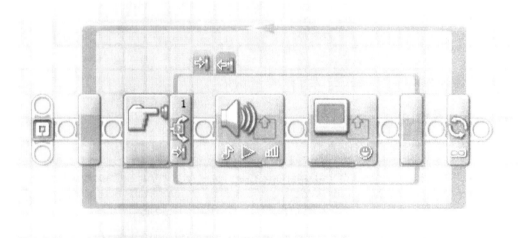

Figure 6-7. Logic on the True beam

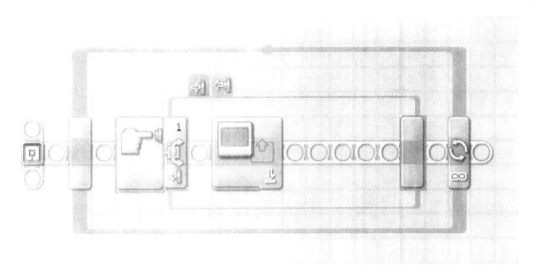

Figure 6-8. Logic on the False beam

Sometimes you may need to evaluate more than just two values, and this is why the tabs come in handy. Say for example you wanted to read the intensity value from a Color sensor and play different tones based on each color read by the sensor. If you simply set the Switch block to use a Color sensor, you'll see that you only get the two options, True or False, based on the color range (see Figure 6-9).

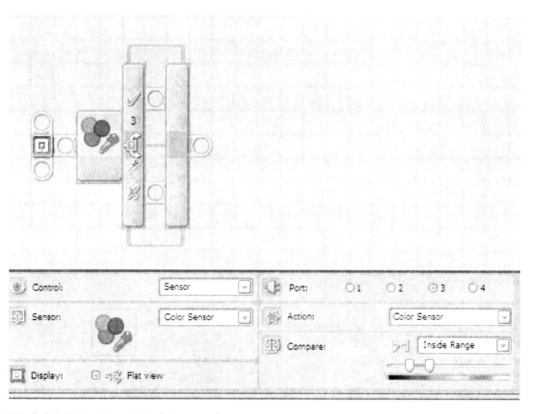

Figure 6-9. Switch block set to evaluate Color sensor

Note The LEGO MINDSTORMS Color sensor ships with the retail version of the MINDSTORMS kit, but are available for individual purchase as well. Currently, the LEGO Color sensor is allowed for use in FLL events. Check with your event rules to see if the Color sensor is allowed.

But what if you want to play a different tone for each color? You will have to change the Switch block to Control from "Sensor" to "Value". You'll notice that in the Properties panel, there is now a list of Conditions. For each condition in the list, a new tab will be added to the Switch block.

The Color sensor has six number values that are associated with detected colors:

    1 = Black
    2 = Blue
    3 = Green
    4 = Yellow
    5 = Red
    6 = White

So you will need to add six conditions to the list to create a tab for each of the detectable colors. To add items to the Conditions list, simply select the Plus button next to the list (see Figure 6-10).

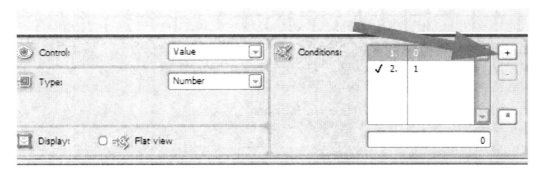

Figure 6-10. Adding items to the Conditions list

In the list, the column on the left contains the condition numbers, and the column on the right contains the value that it will be comparing. So for the Color sensor values, you will need to add the values as ranging from 1 to 6. You can leave a zero value for the default in case no color is detected. In Figure 6-11, you can see that there are seven total conditions in the list: values 1 to 6 are color values and 0 is the default condition.

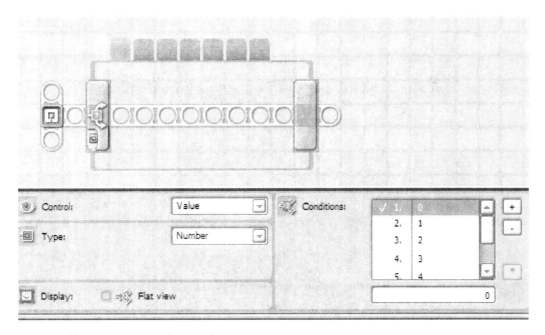

Figure 6-11. Conditions added and tabs increased

> **Note**   To set a value in the Conditions list as the default condition, simply highlight it in the list and select the Asterisk button. A check mark will appear in the left column next to the condition. The default condition will be the tab that is followed in the Switch block when none of the other conditions are met.

Note   By default, the size of the Switch block may be too small to show all seven tabs. Selecting the sequence bar inside the Switch block and dragging to the right will expand the size of the Switch block, allowing you to see all the tabs.

Now that the conditions are configured on the Switch block, an input value needs to be connected via a data wire. Add a Color sensor block and run a data wire from the Detected Color Data Plug to the Value Data Plug on the Switch block. It should look like Figure 6-12 when set up.

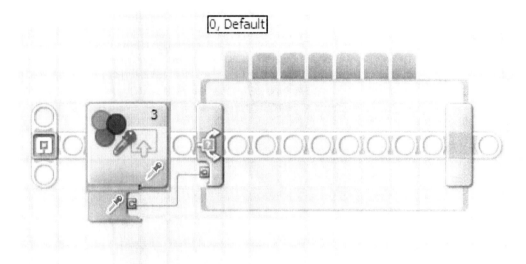

Figure 6-12. Color sensor block wired to Switch block

The next step will be to add some logic to the tabs. Since we want to play different tones based on the color detected, a Sound block should be added to each of the tabs, except the 0 tab since you would not want to play a sound when no color is detected. The tabs should now look like Figure 6-13.

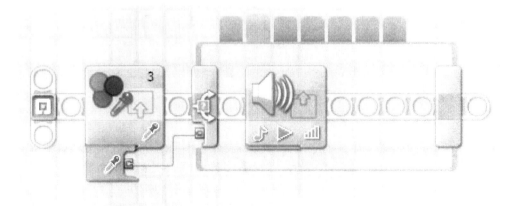

Figure 6-13. Sound block added to the Conditions tab

Be sure to add and set a Sound block on each tab. As you click between the different tabs, you will notice that the sequence bar updates according to the logic associated with that tab.

> **Note** When working a large number of tabs, you will find that the room for error increases because it's easy to forget about a value or logic hidden on one of the tabs.

For this program to work, it will need to be wrapped in a Loop block so that the Switch block can continue to evaluate the Color sensor block value over and over again; otherwise, it will evaluate the sensor value once, and then end the program (see Figure 6-14).

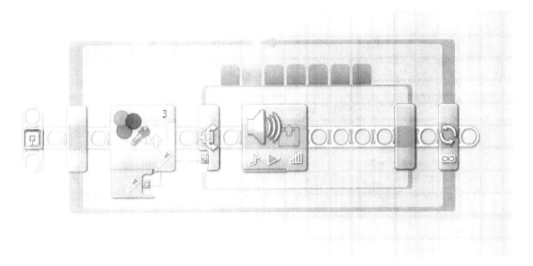

Figure 6-14. Loop block wrapped around the Color sensor logic

If you want to make the program a little more interesting, you could add a display within each tab as well. You could have it play a tone and also display the color's name. So the color red would play an "A" note and display the word "RED" on the NXT screen (see Figure 6-15).

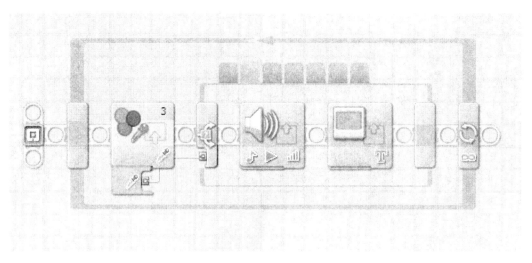

Figure 6-15. Adding a Display block to show the name of the color detected

---

ROBOT HAVING TO THINK FOR ITSELF

Once during a FLL Body Forward game, there was a series of five panels that represented bad and good cells. The panels had black on one side and white on the other. The idea was that you needed to flip black panels to white, but the panels were reset to a random pattern for each match, so there was no way to pre-program a robot to adjust the panels correctly. The robot's program had to be smart enough to evaluate each panel and decide if it needed to be flipped or not.

This was a mission with a big point task, but since it required the use of some conditional logic, many teams ignored the task and left the high-point mission alone. With a simple understanding of Switch blocks, a robot's program could make decisions based on its environment and get some easy points.

Variables

With the Switch block Control property set to Value, you can now evaluate multiple value types from various sources. This gives the Switch block a lot of power when it comes to making choices that affect how your robot will respond to different situations.

Combining the Variable block with the Switch block can become a very powerful tool when you want your robot to think for itself. Say your robot is performing a mission that requires it to change its speed as it approaches a series of parallel black stripes on the game surface. As the number of stripes you pass increases, the speed of the robot needs to slow down and then come to a complete stop once it reaches stripe number 4. But if you don't know what the exact distance is, or maybe it changes every time, you will need a program that can keep track of the number of stripes you have passed and vary the robot's speed based on that value.

So by using a Light sensor, a variable to store the counted lines, and a Switch block, you can allow your robot to determine on its own where and when it needs to adjust its speed.

First, create a variable called **LineCount** with a data type of **Number** (see Figure 6-16).

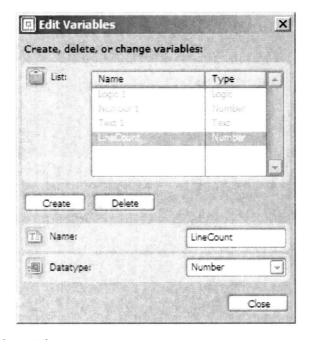

Figure 6-16. *LineCount variable created*

On the sequence beam, set the initial value of the LineCount variable by writing a 0 to the variable with a Variable block, as in Figure 6-17.

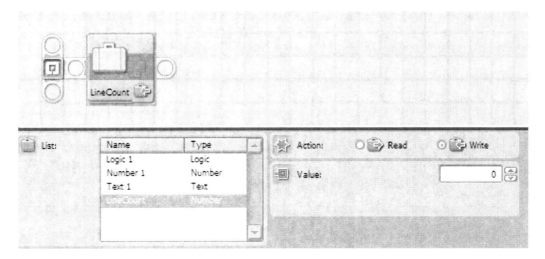

Figure 6-17. *Initializing the LineCount variable*

Then you will add a Move block to start the robot in motion. Follow this with a Loop block that contains a Wait block set for the Light sensor. Your current code should contain what you see in Figure 6-18.

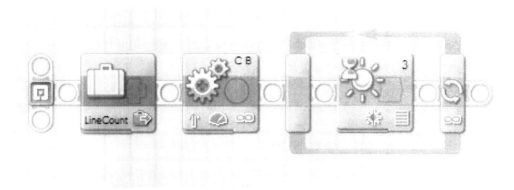

Figure 6-18. Sample code with the Loop block and Light sensor

After the Wait block, you want to increment the LineCount variable by a value of 1. The exiting of the Wait tells you that a black line was seen and that you need to increase the line count to account for the line. In Figure 6-19, you can see that a Variable block value is passed into the Math block, where 1 is added to the current value and then resaved into the Variable block preceding the Math block.

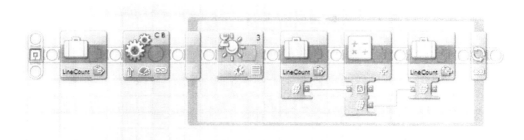

Figure 6-19. Incrementing of the LineCount variable

Before the code looks for another black line, the LineCount variable is evaluated by a Switch block. The Switch block is looking for the number of lines that have been detected. The tabs are set to follow the following values:

Line Count	Motor Power
1	90
2	50
3	30
4	stop

Each tab will contain a Variable block that writes the power value associated with the LineCount condition to a variable called MotorPwr. In Figure 6-20, you can see the tab configuration when the LineCount is equal to three.

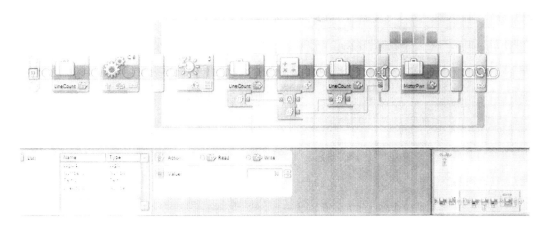

Figure 6-20. *Switch block setting MotorPwr to 30*

At the end of the Switch block, there would be a Move block with the MotorPwr value being passed in as the current value for the robot's motor power (see Figure 6-21).

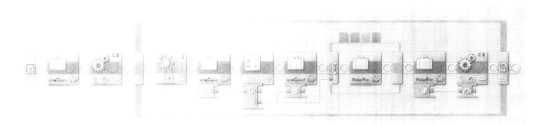

Figure 6-21. *MotorPwr value being assigned to the power property of the Move block*

The Loop block could be set to break out of the loop after the fourth black line is detected as well, so that the LineCount variable will serve two purposes (see Figure 6-22).

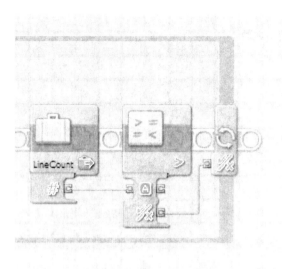

Figure 6-22. Using LineCount to break out of the Loop block

If you have thick black lines, you will have to add some extra logic to the code so that you can detect the starting edge of the black line and the ending edge of the black line. The logic would be as follows:

1.   Move Unlimited.

2.   Wait for Black.

3.   Move Unlimited.

4.   Wait for White.

This approach would work well inside a MyBlock that you create to handle black and white edge detection.

Nesting

Sometimes there is the need to make decisions inside decisions. To do this, you can insert a Switch block inside other Switch blocks; this is called *nesting*. The sequence beam inside the Switch block acts just the same as the normal sequence beam—so anything you can do on one, you can do on the other. Figure 6-23 shows multiple Switch blocks nested together.

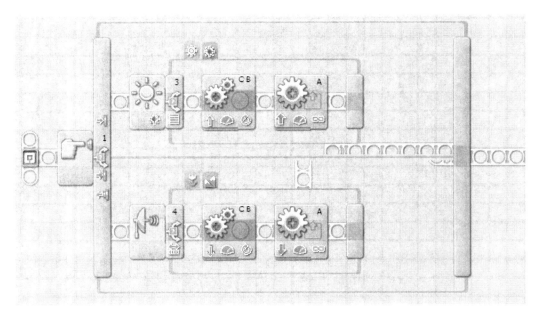

Figure 6-23. Nested Switch blocks

You will notice that multiple Switch blocks can get very confusing to read, and it is tough to follow the program flow. The situation in Figure 6-23 is a good example of when a MyBlock can help with the readability of a program.

Logic Block

One of the more overlooked blocks in NXT-G is the Logic block. This block allows you to compare two logic values (True/False or Yes/No) in various configurations. The Switch block does a simple comparison of a single condition. The Logic block allows you to make multiple comparisons. For example, the Switch block can answer a question such as "Is the Touch sensor on port 1 pressed?," but if you wanted to answer a more complex question such as "Are both Touch sensors on ports 1 and 2 pressed?," you'd need to use a Logic block to make this comparison.

The Logic block has four Operation values:

- Or: If either one of the values is True, then this operation will return a True. Only if both values are False will this operation return a False.

- And: If both values are True, then a True is returned. If any of the values are False, then a False is returned.

- Xor (Exclusive Or): Works similar to the Or, but requires both values to be unique in order for a True to be returned.

- Not: Only checks the Value A being passed to the block, and returns the opposite. So a True returns a False, and a False returns a True.

The Logic block allows for two logical data type values. These can either be input via data wires or set in the Properties panel for the block.

Table 6-1 gives a complete breakdown of how the different operations work based on the input values.

Table 6-1. *Logic Block Value Comparison Table*

Value A	Value B	And	Or	Xor	Not
True	True	True	True	False	False
True	False	False	True	True	False
False	True	False	True	True	True
False	False	False	False	False	True

A good program example would be, let's say, if your robot has two Touch sensors mounted on its rear bumper and you want to know when the robot has squared up to a wall on the game table. If you only check one sensor, your robot might not be completely squared. But you know that when both sensors are pressed, the robot is completely perpendicular to the wall—and you're ready to move on to the next step in your mission.

The program for this would be very hard and messy to write if you didn't have a Logic block—you'd have to have a series of nested Switch blocks, as seen in Figure 6-24. But if you use the Logic block, the code will be much cleaner, as seen in Figure 6-25.

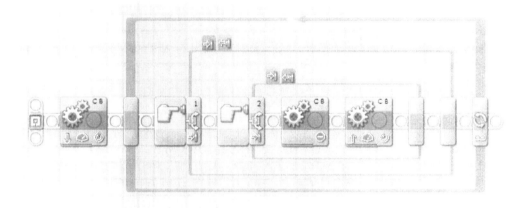

Figure 6-24. *Nested Switch blocks detecting two Touch sensors pressed*

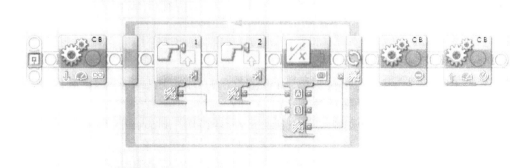

Figure 6-25. *Logic block simplifying the detection of two Touch sensors pressed*

The code logic in Figure 6-25 is easy to read: the robot moves backward toward the wall. Once both Touch sensors are pressed, the program will exit the loop, and then the robot will stop and then move forward.

Compare Block

The Compare block is used to compare two number values. It outputs True or False depending on the condition chosen in the Options panel. For example, you could compare the output from the Ultrasonic sensor to a minimum distance you wish to maintain between the robot and the wall.

The Compare block has three Operation values:

- **Greater Than (>)**: If the Input A value is greater than Input B, the Compare block will return True; otherwise, the value of False will be returned.

- **Less Than (<)**: If the Input A value is less than Input B, the Compare block will return True; otherwise, the value of False will be returned.

- **Equal (=)**: If Input A is the same as Input B, the value of True will be returned.

Figure 6-26 shows a sample program that uses the Compare block with an Ultrasonic sensor to cause the robot to reverse when it gets too close to a wall.

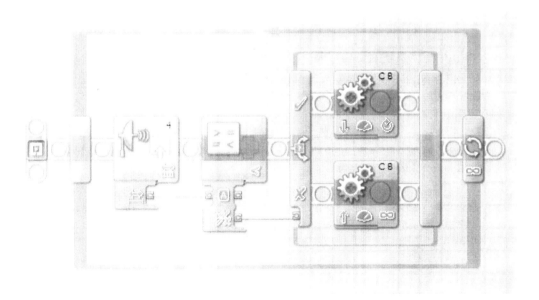

Figure 6-26. A Compare block sample program that will reverse the robot when it approaches a wall

There are alternatives to the Compare block. Many of the other blocks, including the Loop block, Switch block, and the Wait blocks have the same compare functionality included inside of them already. The example shown in Figure 6-26 could have been written using the Ultrasonic sensor compare function built into the Switch block, as seen in Figure 6-27.

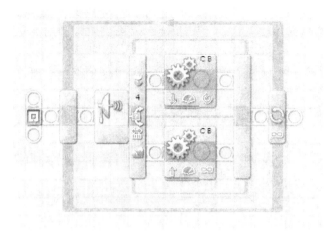

Figure 6-27. A Switch block using an Ultrasonic sensor sample program that will reverse the robot when it approaches a wall

Range Block

The Range block will evaluate a number value and check if it falls inside or outside a given range of numbers. The range values can be hard-coded or wired into the block. Most of the time, the range values are preset in your program while the test value is input via a data wire from another block or variable.

The Operations property of the Range block gives you the following options:

- Inside Range: If the test value is between Value A and Value B, or is equal to either of the values, then the block will return a value of True. This is called an inclusive comparison.

- Outside Range: If the test value is outside the range of Value A and Value B, and does not equal either of the values, then a value of True will be returned. This is called an exclusive comparison.

The example in Figure 6-28 shows the Range block used to see if a Light sensor block has found a gray line. Such a line would have a light range between 1 and 100, so the range values on the Range block are set to 45 through 65, and the Operation property is set to "inside range". If True, the program will play a simple tone with the Sound block.

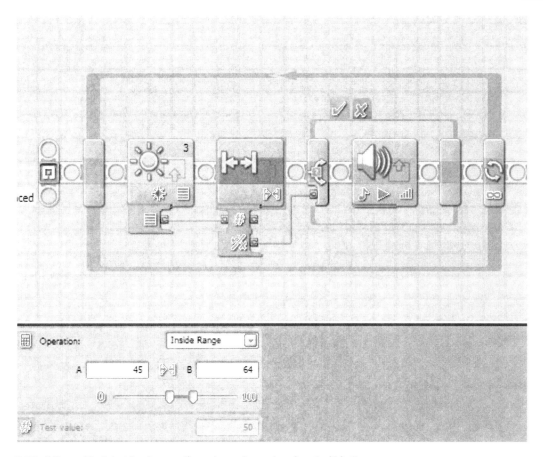

Figure 6-28. A Range block looking for gray lines plays a tone when found within the range

The Range block can come in handy when conditional decisions are not as simple as "Is the value greater than 50?" but are more like "Is the value greater than 80 but less than 30?". Being able to test a range of values comes in very handy in dealing with light intensities. This is demonstrated in more detail in the chapter on light values.

Summary

Mastering the use of these conditional blocks will allow our robot to make smart choices when it's on the game field, giving it the ability to adapt to changes and overcome any unknowns it may run into. Testing and experimenting with the different conditional blocks will give you a better understanding of how each of them can add better decision making to your programs. The ability to display a good understanding of such blocks to a technical judge at an event can help you and your team stand out from teams that are using hard-coded logic in their code.

Chapter 7

Motors and Motion

Once you've built your robot, you're going to want it to go somewhere—and everyone knows the shortest distance between two places is a straight line. In the world of LEGO robots, going straight is one of those things that is easier said than done. Many new teams in FLL will rely on *odometry*, or dead-reckoning, to get their robot to the desired location on the game field.

Odometry is when you use measurements or rotations as a way to navigate your robot to a point on the field. You're simply telling the robot to go a predefined distance, and using the rotation sensors built into your robot's NXT motor to determine if you've gone the desired distance. The position will be measured relative to your starting point. As you will discover, this does not always land your robot where you expected it to end up.

Solely relying on odometry for navigation of your robot is not a good idea; a smart robot will find ways to incorporate landmarks on the game field and be able to analyze where it is in relation to its target using various methods and sensors. It is important to recognize the limitations of the technique, including its risks and to use it only when appropriate. In the FLL Smart Moves challenge, some field items were put in place to purposely limit the use of pure odometry in navigating the missions. So while it can be quick a way to get started on some missions, try not to rely on it too much.

Wheel Circumference

Knowing the circumference of your drive wheels is important when determining how far your robot is going to travel, assuming you are running your wheel directly off the motor, and not going through a series of gears. If you program your Move block to turn four rotations, how far is your robot actually going to travel? This is where knowing your wheel's circumference is important. So now you get to use some math. A basic formula to know is circumference = pi × diameter. The circumference is the distance the wheel will travel after one complete rotation, as seen in Figure 7-1.

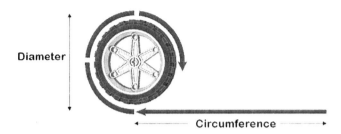

Figure 7-1. Calculating the circumference of a wheel

> **Note** Pi refers to the standard mathematical value by which you multiply the diameter to obtain the circumference. Pi is a never-ending string of decimal digits, but 3.14 is a reasonable approximation.

If your wheel has a circumference of 3 inches and you're moving four rotations, the expected result is that your robot is going to move forward 12 inches (circumference × rotations); or if you need to calculate the number of wheel rotations, then the formula would be duration = distance/circumference. This may seem very straightforward to understand, but so many teams skip right over doing such calculations and just use "trial and error" to get the correct value for their count of the wheel rotations. And then what happens is that something changes with their robot, such as gear ratios or wheel size, and now all their movements are miscalculated and they have to start over with a guessing process to determine the proper rotations.

But if a team understands the math behind calculating the proper rotations from the beginning, then changes will have a very minimal effect on their progress and will not delay the team in moving forward. Also, these are good talking points the team should share with an event's robot design judges. Judges are much more impressed with teams that understand and explain why the robot is performing the way that it is. If a judge asked a team member why the team chose to use four rotations in their program, and the team member simply states that they "just kept trying numbers until something worked," it doesn't sound nearly as impressive as being able to explain the true mathematical reason why four is the correct number of rotations needed for the robot.

Don't forget to take any gear ratios into account when calculating the proper rotation. The *gear ratio* is the value determined by the number of rotations one gear may have in relation to another gear that is driving it. For example, if a small gear is driving a larger gear, the small gear will turn more times than the larger gear. The small gear may turn three times for every single turn of the large gear. Such would be a 3 to 1 ratio, often expressed as 3:1.

In a scenario involving a gear ratio from a driving gear, you would determine the number of wheel rotations using the following formula:

duration = distance ÷ (circumference × ratio)

For example, say that you have a wheel with a circumference of 3 inches that is being driven by a motor hooked to a gear setup with a 3:1 ratio. Your formula would be:

rotation = 12 ÷ (3 × 1/3)

Do the math and you get 12 rotations to travel 12 inches, which is 1 inch per rotation. The multiplication by 1/3 in the formula accounts for the gear ratio, giving a result that you can work with in your motor programming.

Programming to Go Straight

Within NXT-G, there are two blocks you can use for moving your robot in a straight line: the Move block and the Motor block. The Reset Motor block is also helpful, providing a way to reset your rotation count between moves. Finally, you can take advantage of MyBlocks to group all the operations related to a given move by the robot. Doing so simplifies your program and lets you look at things from a more conceptual level.

Move Block

The Move block (see Figure 7-2) in NXT-G would seem to be the obvious solution to programming a robot to travel forward straight, and in most cases this is true. The Move block allows you to control multiple motors at once, and it is designed to keep the rotation of the port B and port C motors in sync using an internal motor synchronization algorithm. This works well on most robot designs and shouldn't be a problem.

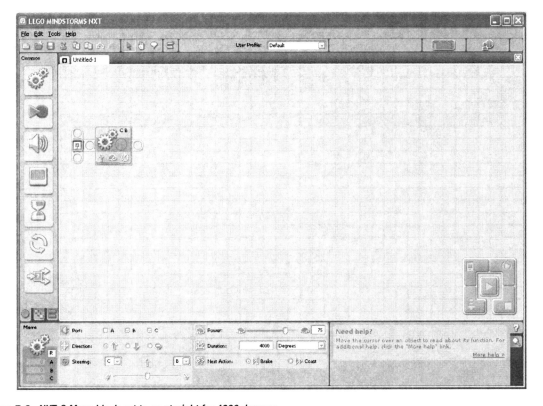

Figure 7-2. *NXT-G Move block set to go straight for 4000 degrees*

One of the things that is missing from the Move block is the ability to control the power ramping for the motors. For example, if you tell your robot to move forward eight rotations with a power setting of 70%, it will run at 70% power until it gets close to the end of the eighth rotation, then it will slow down to avoid overshooting its stopping point. With the Move block, you have no control over this ramping down, so if this is a problem for your desired effect, the Motor block would be a better choice for your program.

Caution   Avoid putting a Move block within a repeating loop. Doing so can cause issues with the Move block maintaining a straight line due to the internal sync logic of the Move block.

Motor Block

The Motor block only allows you to control one motor per block, so to go straight, you would need to include two Motor blocks for each section of code that wishes to move the robot forward in a straight line. It will be important that you keep the two blocks in sync yourself.

For example, if you wish for the robot to travel 5000 degrees forward, you will have to set the distance units on both Motor blocks to be the same. You will also need to tell the first of the two Motor blocks not to wait for completion before running the next block. You do this by disabling the "Wait for Completion" check box. The second block will then need the "Wait for Completion" check box enabled, as seen in Figure 7-3.

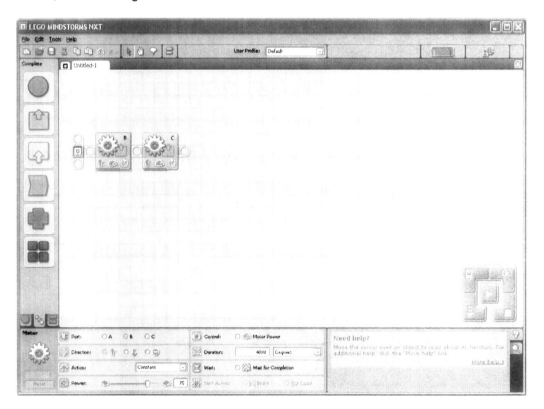

Figure 7-3. NXT-G Motor blocks set to go straight for 4000 degrees

Tip It's a common mistake to omit disabling the "Wait for Completion" feature. If you see your robot spinning in a circle—one wheel turning while the other remains stationary—you may have fallen prey to the mistake. Look to see whether you've unchecked the "Wait for Completion" box.

Unlike the Move block, the Motor block will allow you to specify some ramping up or ramping down.

Reset Motor Block

One of the more underused blocks is the Reset Motor block; executing this block is a great way to help your robot avoid getting confused when running multiple program segments. Executing the block for a motor will reset the motor's automatic synchronization, which is used in blocks like the Move block.

It's a good idea to reset the motors between moves. If your robot seems to get confused about how far it's traveling after running various segments in your program, then using the Reset Motor block between these code segments is a great way to keep things running smoothly. Figure 7-4 illustrates this.

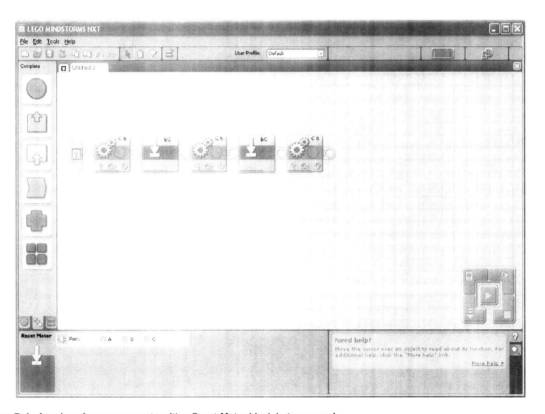

Figure 7-4. A series of move segments with a Reset Motor block between each

MyMove Blocks

The code for moving often involves more than a single block. Using MyBlocks, you can combine all the logic for a given move or type of move into a single unit. You can give that unit a name that makes your code more readable. You can move units around in your code as you troubleshoot and improve your logic.

Consider the task of moving a specific distance in a straight line. One of the things discussed earlier was using the circumference of your robot's wheels and the desired travel distance to figure out the number of rotations your motor needed to turn. To make life simpler, you could add that math into a MyMove block and have the NXT figure out the necessary rotations for you.

Figure 7-5 shows an example. You create three variables: **Motor Power**, **Circumference**, and **Distance**. Motor Power will feed directly into the MyMove block's power wire. Circumference and Distance will feed into a Math block so that you can divide the Distance value by the Circumference to get the necessary rotations for the motor to reach your destination.

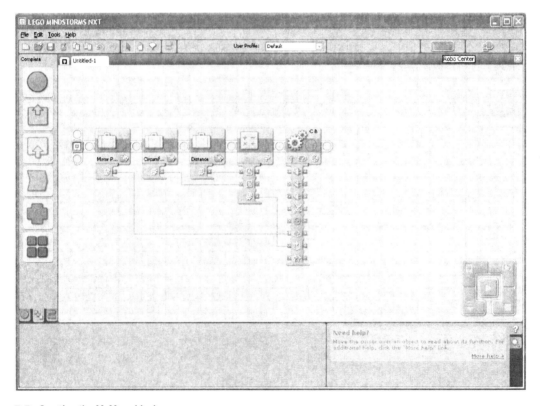

Figure 7-5. Creating the MyMove block

Now that you have your code, you can create the **MyMove** block. When creating a MyBlock that has parameters, you need to be careful when selecting the code that will be included in the actual MyBlock. Leave the variables that will be the parameters out of the selection, as seen in Figure 7-6.

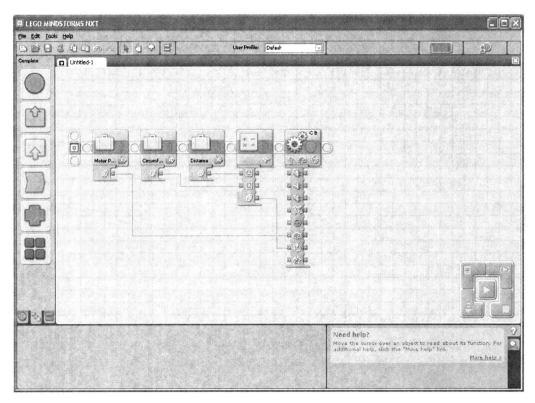

Figure 7-6. Highlighting just the Math and Move blocks—the variables are left out so that they become parameters for your MyMove block

Now that you have the Math and Move blocks selected, you can create the MyMove MyBlock. Figure 7-7 shows that when you created the MyMove block, you ended up with three crosshatch (#) symbols on the left. These represent the three variables that you're using for inputs. They will now show as parameters for the MyMove block, as seen in Figure 7-8.

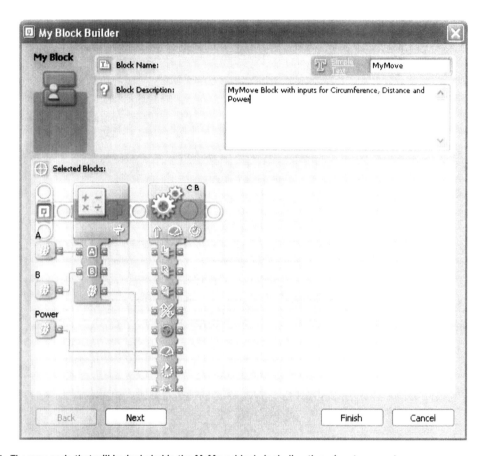

Figure 7-7. *The new code that will be included in the MyMove block, including three input parameters*

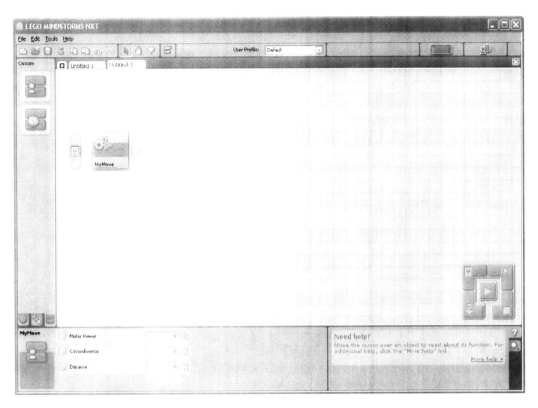

Figure 7-8. The MyMove block now has three input parameters: Motor Power, Circumference, and Distance

It is a good idea to rename the parameters to logic value names so that you will know which values are expected and so that other people who use your block will also understand the values to enter. The default A and B labels don't give a good clue as to which values are expected. Giving the MyBlock a unique icon also helps the user recognize the block visually.

So now you have a reusable MyMove block that can be used in place of a Move block. And the nice thing is that it will calculate the number of rotations needed based on the information you provide to it.

You can build on this and make a MyMove block just for your one particular robot, and then you can hard-code the circumference of your robot's wheels into the MyMove block, and only have to enter the Distance and Motor Power when using the MyMove block. The nice thing about this is that if you changed the wheels on your robot, you'd only have to make the change to the circumference value in your MyMove block to match your new wheel size, and all the programs that use this block would change accordingly. Very simple with no mess.

Turning the Robot

Not only do you need your robot to go straight, but it will need to turn as well. There are various techniques to make your robot turn, as well as different NXT-G blocks that you can use to get it moving in the direction that you want.

Move Block

You learned about the Move block when you wanted to go straight. Now that you want to turn, the Move block can be used again. The Move block has a steering parameter that allows for values between -100 and 100. There is a slider on the block that can move ten positions to the right and ten positions to the left. Each position represents increments of ten. If you wish to enter a value that is not an increment of ten, then you can simply pass it in via the wired parameter.

Table 7-1 presents the key values that are helpful with using the Move block for steering.

Table 7-1. Move Block Common Steering Settings

Steering Value	Steering Results
100	Pivot to the right
50	Turn on one motor to the right
0	Go straight
−50	Turn on one motor to the left
100	Pivot to the left

Other steering values are allowed and can be useful when wanting to travel in a large arc, but they require a bit more trial and error when using the Move block.

Motor Blocks

Using the Motor blocks for making turns can result in turns that are more predictable, but at the same time, teams new to NXT-G sometimes get confused by switching between Move blocks and Motor blocks. So if you're more comfortable with only using the Move blocks, then do what works best for you and your team.

With the Motor blocks, you find that you have more control over your turns simply because you specify the actual power, direction, and duration of each motor. As you saw earlier in this chapter, it's nice to have control over each motor when calculating the durations for your various types of turns.

One trick is to remember that Motor blocks need to be run in sequence, either by branching off a second sequence beam (see Figure 7-9) or by setting the first Motor block in the sequence with the "Wait for Completion" feature turned off (see Figure 7-10).

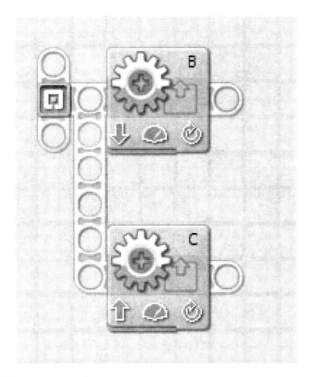

Figure 7-9. Motor blocks on different sequence beams

Figure 7-10. Motor blocks on the same sequence beam

Also be aware that one Motor block may complete before the other, so you will need to let both motor blocks finish before your code moves on to the next statement. Simply adding a slight delay after your move can compensate for this 90% of the time. If you need something more complex, you can simply add some logic that confirms that both Motor blocks have completed their movements before advancing to the next statement in your program.

In Figure 7-11, you can see that each motor will run until competition, then sets the Logic blocks after them to True. The Loop block on the main sequence beam will continue checking both Variable blocks, and loops until both are True. This way, the program knows that both Motor blocks have stopped running.

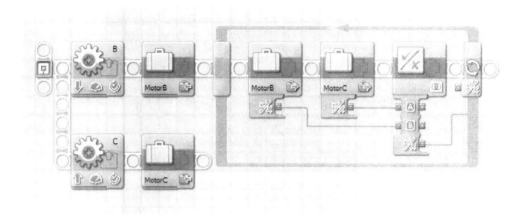

Figure 7-11. Logic added to verify that both Motor blocks have completed running before the program continues executing

Calculating Turns

Most LEGO robots use *differential steering*, which is where the robot controls its turning direction by using two motors, each mounted on either side of the robot. This is the way bulldozers, tanks, and even wheelchairs turn. There are two different ways to turn a differential steering robot—either by turning both wheels or by only turning one wheel and pivoting on the stationary wheel. The trick is to figure out how much you should turn the wheel to get the desired turning position.

Using the upcoming calculations, you will able to accurately calculate the degrees needed for precision turning. Remember though, LEGO robots are based on toys and are not nearly as precise as larger, more expensive robots. So no matter how accurate your math is, the LEGO robots will still need some final tweaking.

> **Note**   There is about 6 to 8 degrees of gear slack—free movement between gears—in a LEGO NXT motor, so getting accurate movements within a few degrees is not possible. Always allow some room for error when turning.

Single-Wheel Turn

If you are turning your robot to the left by only turning the right wheel forward and keeping the left wheel stationary, this will create a steering circle with the left wheel's position as the center (*pivot point*). The distance between the right and left wheel, called the *track*, will be the radius of the steering circle, as seen in Figure 7-12.

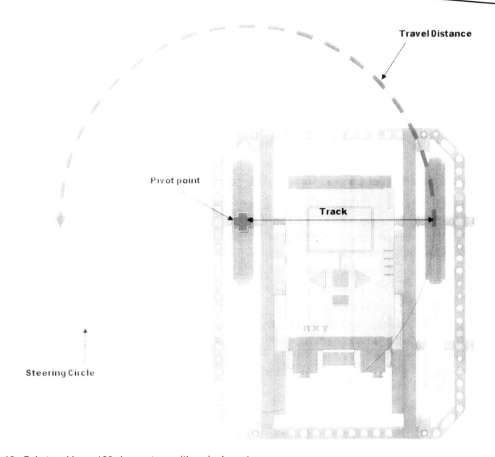

Figure 7-12. *Robot making a 180-degree turn with a single motor*

The circumference of the steering circle is calculated using the following formula:

circumference = 2 × radius × pi

So to turn 90 degrees, your robot would have to travel one quarter of the circumference of the steering circle; whereas a 180-degree turn would require traveling half the steering circle circumference. To calculate the duration needed to use in your Motor block, you would first determine the distance you need to travel around your steering circle. So if you're turning 360 degrees (the complete circle) with your robot, which has a track of 5 inches, the formula would be something like this:

distance = steering circle circumference

distance = 2 × 5 × 3.14

distance = 31.4 inches

With the distance now known, you can calculate the duration needed in your Motor block by using the same formula that you used to calculate the duration when going straight. So if your robot has wheels that have a diameter of 3.25 inches, the formula will look as follows:

duration = distance/wheel circumference

duration = 31.4 ÷ (3.25 × 3.14)

duration = 2.86 rotations

   or

duration = 1029.6 degrees (2.86 × 360)

Now you have found that the number 2.86 is the key. You can multiply this number by any angle turn you wish to make. So if you want your robot to turn 90 degrees instead of 360 degrees, you simply calculate the duration by using your newfound 2.86 key. The duration of a 90-degree turn is calculated as follows:

duration = 2.86 × 90

duration = 257.4 degrees

Even though your key value is unitless, when making these calculations, remember that you keep the units the same for your other values; so if you're measuring your track in inches, the resulting distance will also be in inches. This is the same for the wheel diameter: if all of your other measurements are in inches, then you need to measure the wheel in inches as well.

Dual-Wheel Turn

With the single-wheel turn, your robot is only powering one wheel and turns the robot around an arc. But if you turn both wheels in opposite directions, you can then pivot the robot right where it is sitting. The pivot point is no longer the stationary wheel but the center of the robot's track. You can even use the same calculations used to determine the number of degrees to make the turn in the same way that you did with the single-wheel turn. The only difference is that you will have to divide the degrees in half and apply them to both wheels; one wheel will move in the opposite direction of the other. Figure 7-13 shows how the steering circle is much smaller than the steering circle of a single-wheel turn—actually half the size.

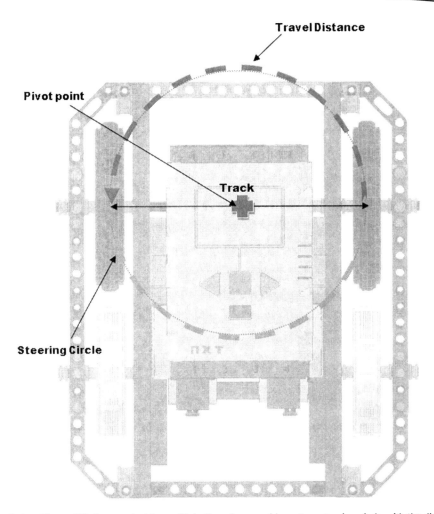

Figure 7-13. *A robot making a 180-degree pivot turn with both motors would create a steering circle with the diameter being that of the robot's track. The center of the steering circle would be the center point of the robot track*

So let's say you want to pivot your robot 180 degrees. Then you would again use the key value that you calculated earlier—2.86—and multiply it by 180, and then divide by 2. You need to divide by 2 since the pivot point is in the middle of the track. Both motors will assist in the turning, so they each only need half as much turning to get the desired duration; for example:

pivot duration = (2.86 × 180) ÷ 2

pivot duration = 514.8 ÷ 2

pivot duration = 257.4 degrees

If we are using a Move block, you set the steering to 100 or -100, depending on which direction you wish to turn, and then enter a duration of **257.4 degrees**, as seen in Figure 7-14. You can also use a pair of Motor blocks—one for motor B and one for motor C. Simply set the duration for both Motor blocks to 257.4 degrees, and then set one Motor block to travel in the opposite direction of the other Motor block. Be sure to either put the block in parallel, or set the first block to not wait for completion, or else the NXT will run the first Motor block and then run the second one, giving you a completely different turn result than you expected (see Figure 7-15).

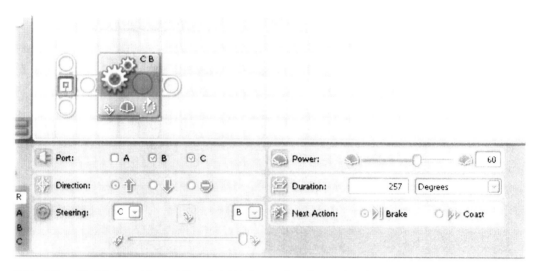

Figure 7-14. A Move block being set to pivot the robot 180-degrees by using a value of 257.4 as the Duration, and the steering set all the way to the far right

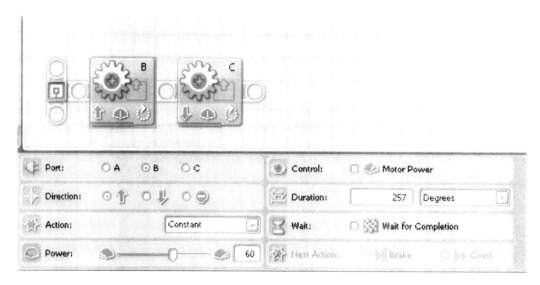

Figure 7-15. Two Motor blocks being set to pivot the robot 180 degrees by using a value of 257.4 as the Duration, and the two blocks turned in opposite directions

Both the Move and Motor blocks work equally well for pivoting. I have always preferred the pairing of the two Motor blocks versus using the Move block—just as a personal preference.

Creating a Custom MyPivot Block

While doing all the calculations for the duration needed to turn in the direction we desire, you may have realized that much of that logic could be included in a custom MyBlock to be used for making a pivot turn. Let's call that new block MyPivot. For example, once you know the key value (2.86 for the robot we just calculated), you could make it a constant in your new MyPivot block, where all you need to do is enter the desired turning degrees and let the block calculate the true duration needed for your robot to complete the turn.

If your robot's wheels or track size change in the future, we simply recalculate the key value and modify the key constant in your MyPivot block without needing to modify any of your code elsewhere. In Figure 7-16, you can see the code that will make up your new MyPivot block. You have a Variable block for your degrees, and a Constant block that will hold your key value of 2.86. These values are then passed to the Math block, where they are multiplied by each other and passed to one more Math block so that you can divide them by 2. The new calculated duration is then passed to a pair of Motor blocks that are running in the opposite direction of each other.

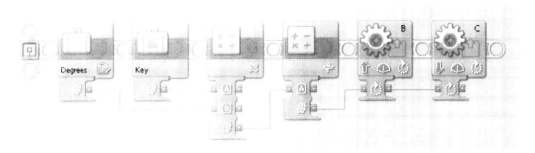

Figure 7-16. *The definition of MyPivot block, which allows the user to pass in the desired turn degrees and have the duration calculated automatically*

To create your new MyPivot block, you will select all the blocks in your code except the Degrees variable, which you purposely leave out of your selection (you'll see why in a moment). Once we have the blocks selected, as seen in Figure 7-17, go to the Edit menu and select "Make a New My Block". Next you will see the My Block Builder dialog box displaying the code that you selected. Now notice that since you did not select the Variable block that contained your degrees value, a special parameter wire was added to your new block. Currently, it is labeled with the letter B, but you can change that later. Figure 7-18 shows the newly created MyPivot block being used with Degrees as the single parameter.

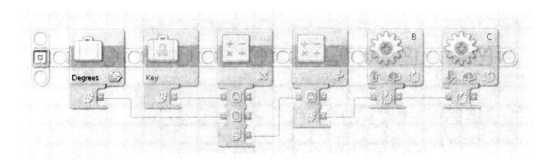

Figure 7-17. Selected blocks that will be a part of your new MyPivot block

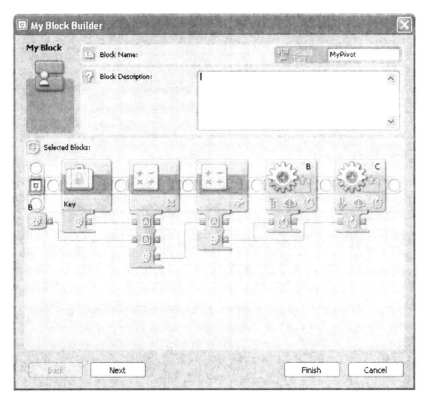

Figure 7-18. The My Block Builder with your code blocks for the MyPivot block. The wired parameter labeled "B" will be your input of degrees

Now when you're done in the My Block Builder dialog box, your newly created MyPivot block will be inserted into your code to replace the code that you selected to be part of the block, as seen in Figure 7-19. The MyPivot block in this example will turn the robot counterclockwise; you can make two versions and change the direction of the two Motor blocks to run in opposite directions. You'll also notice that when you select the MyPivot block, you are presented with one single parameter labeled "B". This parameter is the degrees that we want your robot to pivot.

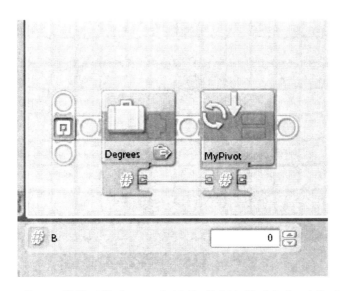

Figure 7-19. Here you can see the new MyPivot block connected to the Variable block that we left out of the MyPivot definition

We could just leave the label set to the letter B as long as we remember what the parameter expects, but to make the best use of your new MyPivot block, we should add the proper label for your own reusability and anyone else on the team that may want to use the MyPivot block.

To change the label, you simply select the MyPivot block and then either double-click the block or select the Edit menu and choose "Edit Selected My Block". The My Block Builder dialog box will open, showing you the code blocks contained within your MyPivot block. If you click on the B label for the input parameter, you can simply type any new label you wish for the parameter; in your case, we'll rename the parameter **Degrees**, as seen in Figure 7-20.

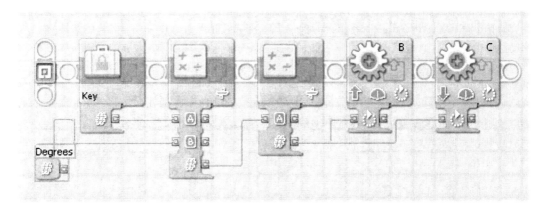

Figure 7-20. Changing the label on the input parameter to read "Degrees" instead of the letter B

Now whenever you use the MyPivot block, the parameter displays as Degrees and makes much more sense to whoever is using the MyPivot block. This helps make the code self-documenting. You can see the results in Figure 7-21.

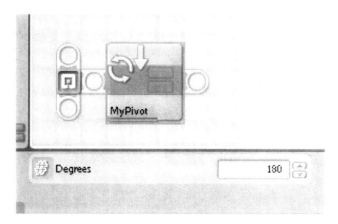

Figure 7-21. *The final MyPivot block with the input parameter properly labeled for easy use and readability*

Creating a Custom MyTurn Block

Let's say that you want a block to do single-wheel turns. You can simply modify the MyPivot block by removing one of the Motor blocks and removing the Math block that divided the calculated value by 2. It would look like what we see in Figure 7-22.

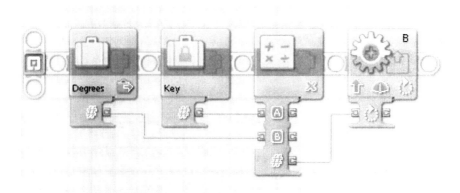

Figure 7-22. *The MyTurn block: similar to the MyPivot block but with only one Motor block and a single Math block*

Now if the Move block is more your style for steering but you'd like to have more flexibility with the steering parameter, you could create a MyMoveSteering block that accepts a parameter value between 100 and -100, thus giving you more control of the steering versus the slider that currently exists in the Move block.

Stall Detection

There are times when you need to run a motor but don't exactly know the distance or duration to run the motor. When you're using a motor to operate a claw attachment, for example, the objects that you're grabbing may vary in size, so sometimes the motor needs to run longer than it does at other times.

If you set the Duration on a Motor block to turn for 90 degrees but the NXT motor is blocked from turning a full 90 degrees, the next block in the sequence will never be executed since the Motor block was not able to complete its action.

A smart solution to this is *stall detection*, which is when your code checks the rotation values of the motor and calculates if the motor is still turning or if it has stopped (or is blocked).

The logic will be simple:

1. Start the motor moving.

2. Take a reading of the motor's position (PosA).

3. Wait a very short time interval.

4. Take a second reading of the motor's position (PosB).

5. Subtract the PosA value from PosB.

6. If the difference is less than 5 degrees, then the motor has stopped turning.

The flowchart diagram in Figure 7-23 shows logic of the stall calculation.

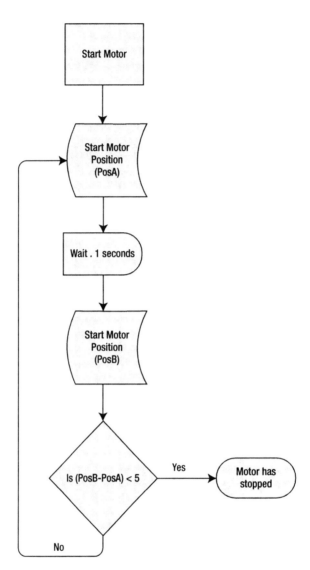

Figure 7-23. Flowchart diagram of the motor stall logic

You can follow the logic in Figure 7-23 by writing a Move block followed by a Loop block that would encapsulate the stall detection logic. Within the loop, monitor the rotation value of the motor. Take a reading. Wait before taking a second reading. Evaluate using a Compare block within a Math block to see whether the rotation varies by more than just a few degrees—say five degrees. If the rotation difference is less than your threshold, then assume that a stall has occurred. Return a value of True to indicate a stall, and False otherwise.

Figure 7-24 shows an example of how to program the stall-detection logic laid out in Figure 7-23.

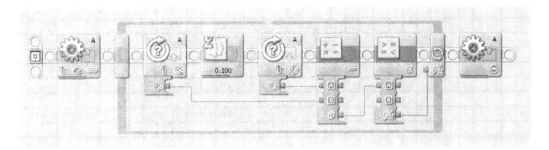

Figure 7-24. Motor stall detection program

Summary

Making your robot perform an action will more than likely involve one or more motors. It is important for you to understand how to make the motor do what you want it to do successfully. Taking some time up front to calculate the proper values for your motor's motion will save you a lot of work later in the design and debug process.

The concepts discussed in this chapter can seem a bit overwhelming, but once you fully understand how to make use of these ideas, you will find that approaching new missions and tasks becomes easier. Don't let the math overwhelm you and just practice the concepts until they make sense.

Chapter 8

Light Detection

A robot that can detect and interpret its surroundings and then make decisions based on those findings is a smart robot. A smart robot is the key to a winning robot. One way for your LEGO MINDSTORMS robot to acquire input from its environment is to use an NXT Light sensor. Many new teams are intimidated to use sensors other than the rotation sensors built into the NXT servos. This doesn't need to be the case.

One of the great things about the NXT Light sensor is that it's a passive sensor as far as hardware. You simply place it on your robot (facing the direction you wish to use for detection) and wire it up. It is ready for action. In order to get the most out of it, you will need to have a good understanding of how the sensor works and what you'll use it for. The ability to develop smart programming code to interrupt the input received from the NXT Light sensor is also important. With that said, our first task in this chapter is to go over just what the Light sensor is and how it works.

NXT Light sensor

The NXT Light sensor allows your robot to visually analyze its environment, basically giving your robot the gift of "sight." Your robot will be able to detect the differences between light and dark, either by detecting the ambient light of its surroundings or by analyzing the color of something in front of the sensor.

> **Note** The LEGO MINDSTORMS Education NXT Base Set (9797) includes one NXT Light sensor. The LEGO MINDSTORMS 2.0 retail set no longer includes the NXT Light sensor but instead has an NXT Color sensor. Currently, FLL rules allow for multiple Light sensors, either the regular or the Color sensors. Be sure to check the rules each year since they are subject to change. Note that only LEGO brand Light sensors are allowed at most LEGO robotics events. There are a few off-brand Light sensors available for the LEGO MINDSTORMS NXT, but these are not allowed in many LEGO robotics events.

How It Works

The NXT Light sensor contains an LED and a *phototransistor* that reads the reflected light from the LED or the ambient light in the room. Ideally, the Light sensor will read from a very narrow field of vision. This field is based on the distance of the sensor from the light source. Pointing the Light sensor at the light fixture on your ceiling gives you a very high-level reading. If you held a black LEGO brick between you and the ceiling light, the sensor would not recognized the brick simply because the field of vision was too great. But if you placed the brick on a table, and pointed and held the Light sensor just a few inches over the brick, it would be able to detect the dark-colored brick. Keep this in mind when placing your Light sensor on your robot's chassis.

Figure 8-1 compares a Light sensor's field of vision when held both close to and far from the LEGO brick. When the sensor is close to the brick, the brick fills the sensor's field of vision. The brick's black color predominates. The Light sensor will return a value indicating darkness.

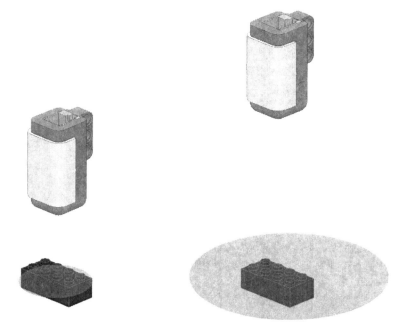

Figure 8-1. *The closer the Light sensor is to an object, the easier it is for the Light sensor to detect the object's light value*

Pull the sensor back, however, and the brick becomes just a small object in a wider field of vision. If the background is light enough, the sensor will not detect the small dark brick against the much lighter background. Detection of the dark brick is more reliable when the field of vision is narrow.

Ambient Light

The Light sensor can measure ambient light when the "Generate light" option is not turned on in the Light sensor block (see Figure 8-2).

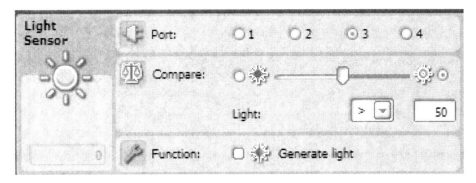

Figure 8-2. *Light sensor properties with the "Generate light" option turned off*

This option turns off the sensor's LED, allowing the light in the room to be the sensor's main source. If you have a robot that needs to detect a dark or bright room, or maybe to determine if it's daytime or night, these types of applications are useful in measuring ambient light. This kind of measurement is rarely necessary or useful in a LEGO robotics event, however. During most robotic competitions, the robot is trying to detect markings on the game field, and not really concerned about the room's lighting.

Reflective Light

We will use the Light sensor for reading reflected light levels—the intensity returned from the surface that the LED light reflects. When properly calibrated, the intensity levels will range from 0 to 100, but when you look at the noncalibrated values of the Light sensor, you will see that the range is much smaller, more like 30 to 70. This is because the Light sensor can read a much wider spectrum of colors beyond what our human eye can see. So the calibration process puts the values into a range that you can find useful.

Calibration

When using the Light sensor as an input source, you learn quickly that ambient (or background) light varies from place to place. The light in your classroom or basement may be quite different from the light where a robotics event is being held. So the idea behind calibration is to adjust your sensor to the conditions expected in the room.

Depending on the room, you may only need to calibrate once in the room that you run your robot, even if you are running it multiple times within the same day. But if the room has lighting conditions that change, such as large windows that bring in natural sunlight, you may want to calibrate your NXT Light sensors before every run. Proper shielding of your Light sensors is also important for getting consistent light-sensor readings. Anything you can do with your robot design to prevent outside light from interfering with your sensors is helpful.

Don't start calibrating your sensors until you have them positioned on your robot's chassis. Changing the sensors' locations on the chassis can affect the value readings. Ideally, you're going to want to keep your NXT Light sensors close to the game field; around 2 to 3 centimeters is a safe distance. But make sure your robot can clear any obstacles that it may have to climb. You don't want your robot getting caught on the sensor because of low ground clearance.

You need to calibrate your sensor so that you can set the real-world values for lightness and darkness. In the ideal environment, the NXT believes white to be the maximum value returned and black to be the minimum value returned. These values are represented in the NXT-G code as values between 0 and 100, but rarely will an uncalibrated sensor ever return these values—most of the time the real values return within a range of 30 to 70. By calibrating the NXT, we are resetting the limits of the light reading range based on light readings in the current environment. Also, calibrating the Light sensor allows the robot to run in different environments without having to change the program code to contain the new room's light values.

LIGHTING AT EVENTS

One year I was at an FLL qualifier held in an airplane hangar. The location was great, but the lighting was horrible for robots. Every game table in the room had different lighting contrast. This was an excellent opportunity to have a robot that would calibrate its light on each run. Too bad our team didn't have such a calibration plan at the time. We got lucky and had a very good run on a table with consistent lighting. Our other runs that day were not as impressive.

Look out for rooms that have lots of natural sunlight coming through windows. I've seen events where the sun in the room changed throughout the day, and robots that ran flawlessly early in the day had issues as the lighting changed.

You can perform the calibration in two ways: by using NXT-G's own Light Calibration block that stores the calibrated values in the NXT's memory or by creating your own calibration program that stores the values locally in a file on the NXT.

NXT-G Calibration Block

In the NXT-G Advanced Tools menu, there is a Calibration block that is used to calibrate the maximum and minimum levels for both the NXT Light and Sound sensors. The values read by the Calibration block are stored on the NXT brick and remain until they are deleted or the sensors are recalibrated, even if the NXT brick has been turned off.

If you are using two NXT Light sensors on your robot, the calibration values stored by the Calibration block will be applied to both sensors. The NXT does not store separate values for each sensor.

To use the Calibration block, you simply add it to your NXT-G program. Most likely it is in a separate calibration program or at the beginning of the program that you are about to run. If you wish to include it in all of your programs and calibrate before each run, creating a MyBlock with your calibration code is a good idea. Be sure to verify with your event coordinator about when and where calibration is allowed.

You could create a My Calibration block, for example. Within this block, you would have to include two Calibration blocks—one to read the minimum light value and one to read the maximum light value—and some kind of trigger event, such as a Wait block, between the two Calibration blocks. For example, the first Calibration block reads the maximum light value, waits for the NXT orange button to be pressed, and then reads the minimum light value. When you first run this program, you hold the robot's Light sensor over the lightest surface on the game field, preferably a part of the mat that is white (or a very light color). Next, you move the robot's Light sensor over a dark area of the mat in order to read the minimum value. Then, you press the orange button on the NXT brick (see Figure 8-4). Figure 8-3 is a simple example of such a calibration program. You might want to elaborate on it by adding display prompts to let the user know where he should place the robot's Light sensor and what to do next.

Figure 8-3. A simple NXT-G calibration program

If you attach your NXT brick to your computer via a USB cable or Bluetooth, and then select Calibrate Sensors from the Tools menu in the NXT programming software, you are prompted by a dialog box to download an NXT-G calibration program. This program works very similarly to the one described earlier and it already has all the prompts in place for easy use.

Figure 8-4. *Calibrating the Light sensor over a light-colored area and a black line*

Local File

You may not wish to use the Calibration block that comes with NXT-G. Your robot may have two Light sensors, for example, and you want to store a separate calibration value for each sensor. You can do this by creating your own calibration program and then storing the values in a text file on the NXT brick. By saving to a file, you are able to read that file and retrieve the stored light calibration values each time your programs are run.

The process I've described is really not as complicated as it sounds. It can be made into a really nice program without much effort or code. In Figure 8-5, you can see that the Calibration block is replaced with a Light sensor block that copies a value from the Intensity into a text file. If you are using multiple Light sensors, you could do the same process for each sensor, thus allowing you to have a unique light range for each. When using the NXT-G Calibration block, the value calibrated is applied to all Light sensors connected to the NXT brick.

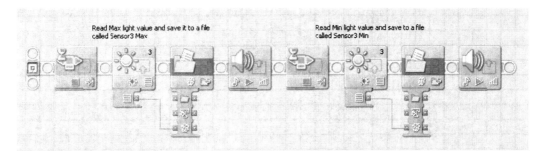

Figure 8-5. *An NXT-G calibration program that writes the max and min values to a text file*

To use the values that you saved, your line-following program would first read the saved values in the files, and then calculate the desired light value range. This would require a bit more math for a Conditional line-following program, but would fit right into our Proportional line follower that is covered next.

Viewing Calibration

One thing that confuses people about calibration is the newly calibrated values. The NXT has a built-in utility that allows you to view the values of its various sensors; but the NXT always displays the uncalibrated values of the Light sensor. So if you use the Calibration block and store new calibration values for the NXT Light sensor in the NXT's memory, and then try out the built-in Light sensor viewer on the NXT, it will not show you the newly calibrated values, it continues to display the original uncalibrated values.

To work around this problem and be able to see the real values, we write our own Light sensor value viewer that will show us the calibrated values being returned from our Light sensor. It's important for us to know these values so that when we start writing our line-following routines, we know the proper range values that our robot will be attempting to detect.

The program is simple, as you can see in Figure 8-6. You create a loop that contains a Light sensor block and that is wired to a Number to Text block. This converts the numeric value returned from your Light sensor to text so that it displays on your NXT screen. The converted value is now passed to the Display block. Wait a moment before taking another Light sensor reading.

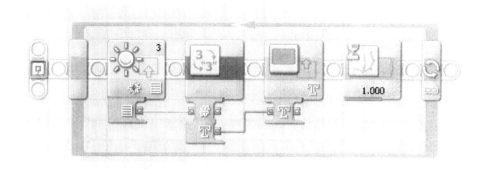

Figure 8-6. A calibrated light value viewer to display the calibrated Light sensor value on the NXT screen

A program like this is very helpful in figuring the initial range for your line-following program, when you're debugging your program, and for experimenting with different Light sensor positions on your robot's chassis. You can move the Light sensor around to get a feel for the difference in light readings based on things such as distance from the game field or even various light sources in your room.

You may find it helpful to run a viewing program while shining various light sources at your robot as it sits on the game field. You can discover how different kinds of light have an effect on your readings. Try the lights at various angles (shadows often cause more issues that the light itself).

Deleting Calibration

The NXT-G Calibration block has a delete function that clears out any calibrations currently stored in the NXT brick's memory. It is wise to clear out such values at the beginning of your calibration process—just so you know you're working with clean values in your NXT brick, especially if you're in a classroom where different people are sharing an NXT brick.

Figure 8-7 illustrates a basic Calibration deletion program. First, the program waits for the user to press the orange NXT button, then it deletes the current calibration with the Calibration block, and then it plays a confirmation tone.

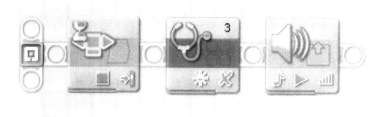

Figure 8-7. A program to delete the current Light sensor calibration

Line Following

A great way to navigate *along* the field is to follow any lines that may be present on the field map. In FLL, for example, the 2009 Smart Moves field was a line follower's dream. There were nice thick black lines that could guide a robot to most of the important places on the field. Actually, it was done to encourage teams to incorporate line following, or at least line detection, in their robot's logic.

A lot of teams recognize this but struggle with how to build and develop a good line-following robot. The code doesn't have to be scary. Yes, you can have some very complicated line-following logic and use lots of fancy algorithms to keep your robot traveling smoothly, but at the same time, there are simple solutions. There are multiple techniques available for getting your robot to follow a line. Remember, though, that the techniques described in this section are just examples. You and your team are encouraged to use them as a starting point, but then build on the techniques and see how much better you can make them.

Simple Condition

The simplest of line-following programs is a dual-state program in which the Light sensor either sees black or white, and adjusts accordingly. The robot oscillates back and forth over the line, constantly checking for either black or white values; even if the line is straight, the robot will continue to move back and forth searching for the line. The robot is looking for two conditions—the light value is either dark or is bright—and based on these values, the robot will go either to the right or to the left. So the robot is only working in a mode with two conditions (dark or bright) and two actions (turn left or turn right).

This kind of program is a good start for teams just learning line following and trying to get a grasp on the robot and the code. Most advanced teams use something a bit more complex, or at least smoother running. The more the robot oscillates, the slower it performs, so ideally the robot will run as straight as possible when navigating a line.

The code for such logic is fairly simple, as seen in Figure 8-8. The assumption is that your robot is only using one NXT Light sensor at this point. The example in Figure 8-6 shows a master loop that runs continuously. In a real-world situation, you would need to include some kind of condition that breaks the robot out of the loop in order to continue to the next step in the competition. But for this example, having the robot stay in a constant line-following mode is fine.

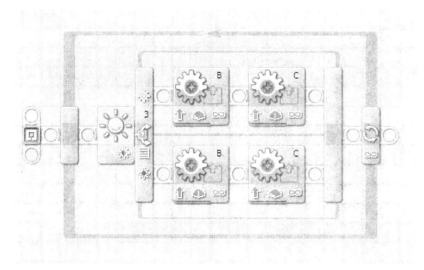

Figure 8-8. *A simple line-following program that zigzags back and forth over the line*

You will have a Switch block that is using a Control type of sensor. The sensor will be your Light sensor. You will also need to configure the port that the Light sensor is connected to on your robot. In Figure 8-8's example, the Light sensor is connected to port 3.

Assuming that the robot's Light sensor has been calibrated at this point, your Compare value for the Switch block will use 50 as the middle point. So if the light value returned is less than 50 (darker), you will turn the robot to the left—looking for a value that is greater than 50 (lighter). You can see that the power settings on the Motor blocks differ depending on which direction you wish to turn. In Figure 8-8, the motor's power settings are 50 for the higher value and 20 for the lower. Depending on your robot's design, you may need to adjust these values so that your robot doesn't turn too sharply. Then you'll loop back and check the Light sensor value again. There is no condition that allows your robot to move perfectly straight. It will always go to the left or the right as it moves forward.

This program is not following the line itself so much as the edge of the line. It tries to stay on the left edge of the line. If our line has lots of arcs to the right, you might want to switch up the program and follow the right edge of the line instead since any sudden changes in the direction of the line could cause this simple program to miss the line and end up in never-never land. This type of program works best with lines that stay relatively straight or only curve slightly. Lines with intersections are more difficult to detect with such a simple technique—they require a more complex solution, as described next.

Complex Condition

With the Simple State example, the program only had two conditions: a light value either greater than or less than 50. The problem is that the robot tends to overcompensate for changes in the light value. Think of a car that has a tire go off the roadway. If the driver turns the wheel drastically to the left, he will bring the car back onto the road—but he could very well cause the car to lose control and run off the other side of the road. So the driver *gradually* turns the car back toward the road.

He remains in control of the car since the compensative reaction was in relation to the amount of error needing correction.

You can do the same thing with your LEGO robots by adding more conditions to the switch logic. The value returned from a calibrated Light sensor is between 0 and 100. If the value is close to 0, we want to make a more drastic change in direction compared to a value around 35, where we'd only need a slight correction in direction. So we divide our possible light range (0–100) into smaller sections. Create five series of smaller ranges by dividing 100 by 20. This gives us the new condition values that we will use in our Switch block. Table 8-1 presents the code that we use for each condition in our code.

Table 8-1. Complex State Conditions

Range Value	Action
0	Sharp Turn to the Left: slow down motor B.
1	Slight Turn to the Left: slow down motor B slightly.
2	Stay Straight: keep both motors equal.
3	Slight Turn to the Right: slow down motor C slightly.
4	Sharp Turn to the Right: slow down motor C.

The example code seen in Figure 8-9 contains a master loop that runs continuously with a Light sensor block. The Intensity value from the Light sensor block is wired to a Math block in which we divide the Intensity value by 20 and the result is rounded off to the closest value. This value is what we pass to the Switch block. Since it is possible to get a return value of 5, when the light value is higher than 90, simply set your condition 4 as the default condition on the Switch block—thus forcing the condition 5 to use the same actions as the condition 4.

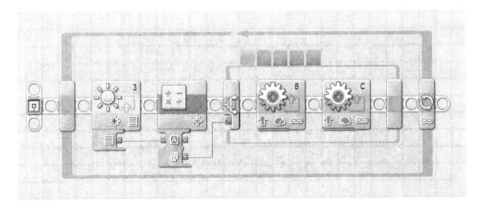

Figure 8-9. Complex condition line-following program with five conditions in the Switch block

Within each condition of the Switch block, the Move blocks are set at various power levels to force the robot to turn in one direction or the other; but when the condition value is 2, both Motor blocks are set to the same power level to allow the robot to travel straight.

Proportional

To make the turns even smoother, take the Complex state method and further break down the Light sensor Intensity value from five conditional states to ten. This may be a bit much to manage in NXT-G. Large Switch blocks can become very clumsy in the NXT-G interface.

Whenever you talk to anyone about robotics and line following, the term "PID" comes up. It stands for **p**roportional-**i**ntegral-**d**erivative. Most LEGO NXT-G programs that people claim are PID are really just P. For NXT-G, a proportional type of program is very doable, whereas a full PID is a bit much for such a simple programming language. A proportional system uses a bit of math to calculate the amount of correction needed to return the robot back to the line that it is following. So instead of using a set value to correct the robot's direction, we calculate the direction change based on the value read by the Light sensor. If the error value is small, then the robot corrects very slightly; if the error is large, the robot must heavily correct.

For our example Proportional NXT-G program, we start with a few Variable blocks, as described in Table 8-2.

Table 8-2. *Variable Definitions Used in the Proportional Line-Following Program*

Variable	Description
MidRange	The mid value between the minimum and maximum light readings. If the Light sensor is calibrated with a minimum value of 0 and a maximum of 100, the MidRange is 50.
Gain	Used to fine-tune our error correction. If the robot is zigzagging too much, set the Gain to a value lower than 1. If the robot is not responding fast enough, set the Gain a bit higher to adjust the correction.
Power	The power that the robot travels at when going straight. This value should be adjusted between 30 and 70, depending on your robot's design. Be careful not to set the value too high, or else the robot might miss the line.
Error	A value calculated by the MidRange from the light value intensity. The Error is used when we set the Correction to the robot's motors.
Correction	The Gain applied to the Error amount. It gives the difference to apply to the Power variable, which is then applied to the motors.

The logic in your code is fairly simple (see Figure 8-10). First, calculate the Error correction value by subtracting the MidRange value from the Intensity value returned from the Light sensor. Next, calculate the Correction value by multiplying the calculated Error by the Gain. The Correction value will be applied to the Power value and then passed to the Motor block. The trick is to invert the value between the two motors. So for Motor block B, add the Correction to the Power. For Motor block C, subtract the Correction from the Power. In Figure 8-8, this logic is put into an NXT-G program. Remember that robot designs require adjustments to the Power, Gain, and MidRange, depending on the robot's response. Also remember that you are following the edge of the line. In this example, you're following the left edge. If you wanted to follow the right edge, you would simply reverse the addition and subtraction.

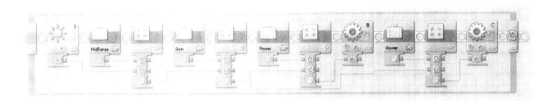

Figure 8-10. *The Proportional line-following program does not use a Switch block; instead, it calculates the necessary power to drive the motors and keep the robot on the line*

Dual Light Sensors

So far, the examples have dealt with robots that only use a single Light sensor to detect the edge of the line. But what if you added a second Light sensor and straddled the line? The FLL rules allow for two Light sensors even though the LEGO MINDSTORMS kits do not include a second sensor. You can purchase them separately if desired.

When you have two Light sensors, you want them to be spaced on your robot just a bit wider than the line it will try to follow. If the sensors are spaced too close together, you'll never get a valid state for going straight; if they are too far apart, you will find your robot overcompensating direction changes when it hits the line. Ideally, neither sensor should see the line when the robot is centered over the line; they should only see the area next to the line.

If you want to use the Complex state method that we discussed earlier, you simply add a second Switch block, one for each Light sensor and motor. Each Light sensor is isolated to the motor on its side of the robot. Each Switch block has only three conditions, as seen in Table 8-3, Figure 8-11, and Figure 8-12's robot with dual Light sensors.

Table 8-3. *Complex State Conditions for Dual Light-Sensor Robots*

Light Sensor	Range Value	Action
Left	0	Sharp Turn to the Left: slow down motor B.
Left	1	Slight Turn to the Left: slow down motor B slightly.
Right/Left	2	Stay Straight: keep both motors equal.
Right	1	Slight Turn to the Right: slow down motor C slightly.
Right	0	Sharp Turn to the Right: slow down motor C.

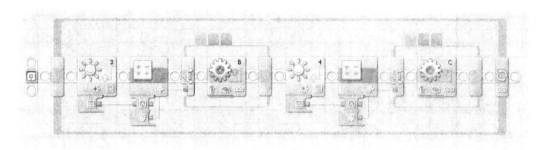

Figure 8-11. Complex condition line-following program: a Switch block for each Light sensor and only three conditions

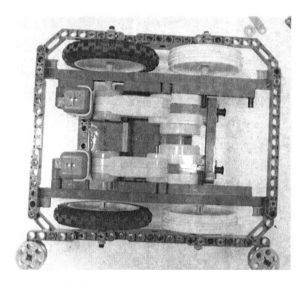

Figure 8-12. A robot with dual Light sensors installed

For this approach to work properly, both Light sensors need to straddle the line. If the robot gets into a position where both Light sensors see black, the robot simply slows down because the conditional switches slow both motors from trying to force the robot to turn. This can happen when a robot leaves the base and is expecting a line to follow just outside the base. Since the robot detects the border around the base, you can do one of two things: add a delay to the program to prevent line detection when the robot leaves the base, or allow the robot to slow down when it first detects the border, and then have it speed up again after it is past the border around the base.

Line Detection

The lines on a game field can serve uses for navigation beyond line following. Many times, various areas on the game field are outlined by a line or box of some sort. The line may not be a true line, but rather a shape or an image. These shapes and images are still important and can be very helpful when trying to determine if your robot is in the right location. Be aware that these lines may not be simple black lines. Many times they are colored lines and require a bit more effort to detect properly with an NXT Light sensor.

In the 2008 FLL Climate Connections game field shown in Figure 8-13, parts of the field are outlined with various colored lines. These were very useful for trying to navigate to a given area to perform a task. What made them tricky was that they were colored lines and that you had to cross over a large rainbow printed on the mat. The job wasn't as simple as driving forward until you saw a red line. You had to time when the robot began looking or you had to count the number of red lines you encountered.

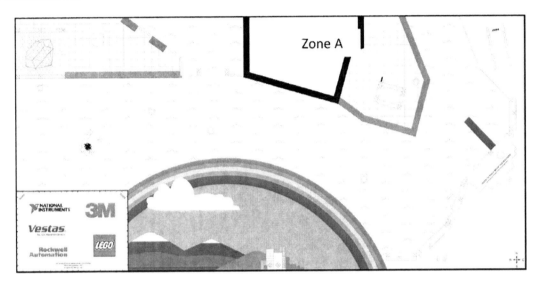

Figure 8-13. *The 2008 FLL Climate Connections field mat*

Finding the Line

If you look at Figure 8-13, you see that it doesn't have many lines that would be helpful for line following, but there are lots of thick lines that either outline or could guide a robot to a particular location on the field. These lines are there to help a robot navigate to particular locations. In the middle of the field is a lot of open space. It would be very easy for a robot to get lost in this space. The borders help a robot know when it has reached the desired location.

Let's say your robot leaves base and is heading to the location labeled "Zone A". After the robot leaves base, it is very dependent on odometry to find its way across the field. During this time, it should use its Light sensor to look for the thick black border around Zone A. You will have to be careful that the other colors on the field don't confuse it—that rainbow has tripped up many robots. These are things that you need to consider when planning the task for your missions. What things may be in your way? What other markings on the mat can confuse your robot?

Now look at the 2007 FLL Power Puzzle field mat in Figure 8-14. It is very different from the Climate Connections mat in that it has well-defined zones with easy-to-track borders.

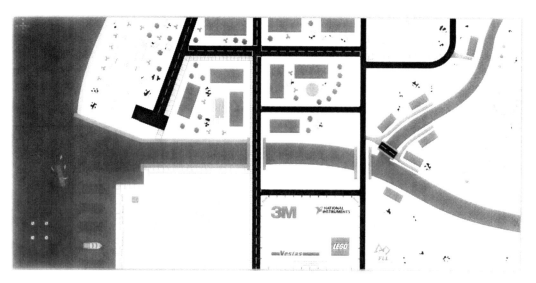

Figure 8-14. The 2007 FLL Power Puzzle field mat

There are a few roads that you can use for line following and the blue rivers are great for breaking up the different areas of the mat—giving your robot quick feedback on where it is located on the field. Down the middle there are three distinct black lines crossing the robot's path as it leaves base heading north. These lines are great for counting and helping the robot learn where it is located. When you count lines, remember that you cannot merely count the number of times your Light sensor sees a black line. As a Light sensor travels over the line, it reads it multiple times because the sensor is very fast. You will have to include logic in your code to first look for a black line, and once found, increment the counter to look for the color white. Once white is found, look for black again. This process continues for however many lines you're expecting to encounter. Figure 8-15 illustrates an example of such code in NXT-G.

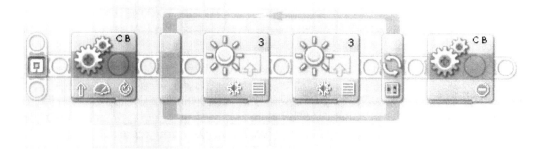

Figure 8-15. NXT-G line-counter code

Reading Colored Lines

Many of the lines or areas that you encounter are not simple black-and-white lines; many of them are colored lines or edges. Even though we're using the NXT Light sensor and not the NXT Color sensor, we can still detect different colors.

Ideally, you will still be able to calibrate your Light sensor on a white-and-black source. The color values will fall between the calibrated ranges of 0 and 100. It is best to first calibrate your Light sensor. Then run the light value view program, place your Light sensor over the various colors on the game field map, and record the values you read for each color. As long as you can calibrate your robot consistently, the color values should read the same.

Be careful! Some colors will share the same value. Many times red, green, and gray return the same Intensity values to the NXT Light sensor. This is why it is important to get a good reading on each color and keep track of which values register the most consistent results.

When you are thinking through your strategies for navigating the field, look for colors that contrast more drastically with other colors to help avoid confusion and make finding the navigation points easier. Thick lines are going to make better markers than thin or fuzzy lines and edges, of course. You really want anything that is unique and can produce consistent readings back to your program. Consistent markings produce consistent results.

Aligning with Lines and Edges

In addition to the table walls, most game fields have some type of printing or markings on the field that your robot can use for alignment. The trick in making use of these markings is to use a second NXT Light sensor.

Aligning the robot using field markings can be very effective and give you a bit more flexibility than solely relying on the table walls. Ideally, your robot will take advantage of both types of squaring. With field markings, you can align the robot with various angles, depending on the markings on the field. On the 2008 FLL Climate Connections game field you can see that the different areas have thick-colored lines outlining them. If used correctly, these lines are great for helping line up a robot for various missions.

We will use these colored lines for lining up as we do with the walls, but instead of the ability to push up to a wall, we need to have smart code for our NXT to recognize that we are at a line and determine which direction the robot needs to turn to align itself with the line or marking. You will have two NXT Light sensors mounted parallel with each other on the robot. They need to be as wide apart as possible on the chassis.

The reason for having the sensors far part from each other is to prevent the robot's turns from being drastic when lining up. Having the sensors far apart allows for a smooth and precise alignment. The closer together the sensors are located, the faster the second sensor will approach the line edge as the robot turns to square itself to the line. This will begin to make more sense once you learn more about the logic involved to turn the robot. Keep reading!

Your robot will have the two Light sensors on. It will be searching for the color line that you have programmed the robot to expect. For example, say the mission we're going to tackle has a black line in front of it. A black line will register a low number reading on the Light sensor. So our NXT-G code, as seen in Figure 8-16, will tell each Light sensor to be on the lookout for a light reading with a low number, maybe 30 or lower depending on whether there is other printing on the field that we need to be concerned about. We don't want to trigger a false positive on something that is not our line.

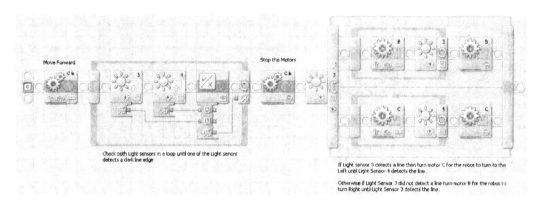

Check both Light sensors in a loop until one of the Light sensors detects a dark line edge

If Light sensor 3 detects a line then turn motor C for the robot to turn to the Left until Light Sensor 4 detects the line.

Otherwise if Light Sensor 3 did not detect a line turn motor B for the robot to turn Right until Light Sensor 3 detects the line.

Figure 8-16. An NXT-G program using NXT Light sensors to align the robot with a line detected on the game field

The robot is running along when the Light sensor on its right side detects a black line. Now we need to find that line with the left Light sensor. All the robot has to do is stop moving forward and turn to the right until the left Light sensor also detects the line. Once both Light sensors have found the edge of the line, the robot should align with the line.

Your robot is using the first Light sensor that detected the line as a pivot point. It will now turn along the pivot point until the other Light sensor reaches the line, as seen in Figures 8-17 and 8-18.

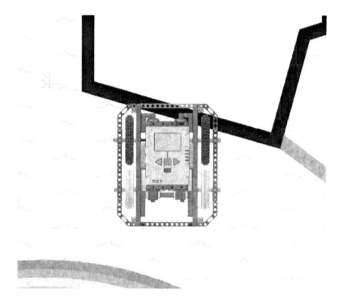

Figure 8-17. The first sensor detects when the robot encounters the line

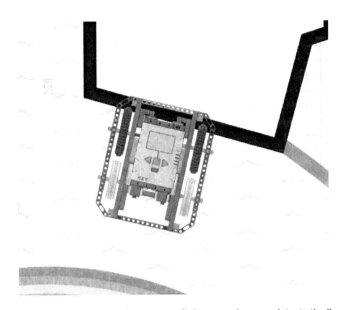

Figure 8-18. The robot then pivots on the first sensor's corner until the second sensor detects the line

Having the Light sensors a good distance apart from each other ensures that you get a straight alignment with the line. If the sensors are too close together, it leaves more room for error in making proper alignment.

Summary

Using and understanding lights and Light sensors can contribute to making your robot better navigate the field. They allow your robot to make smart decisions based on its environment.

Don't be intimidated by the use of Light sensors. There can be a slight learning curve, but with some practice and lots of experimenting, you will find that the Light sensor is one of the best tools in your toolbox when it comes to building a winning LEGO robot.

Chapter 9

Touching and Bumping

As I've stated, a smart robot is one that fully uses its sensors. One of the simplest, most useful sensors is the Touch sensor, shown in Figure 9-1.

Figure 9-1. LEGO MINDSTORMS NXT Touch Sensor

The Touch sensor allows your robot to "feel" its way around a course and react appropriately. It is very basic—it's either on or off, depending on the state of the Push button. The Touch sensor provides a hole for an axle in the Push button—giving users more options for incorporating the sensor into their designs.

The Touch Sensor

The Touch sensor reports its status to the NXT as one of three states: Pressed, Released, or Bumped. You see these in the Properties window shown in Figure 9-2.

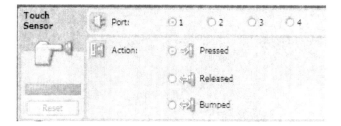

Figure 9-2. The Touch Sensor Properties window

If there is no action or force placed on the button at the front of the sensor, the sensor reports its state as Released. If force is held on the button, then the state of the sensor is Pressed. If the button is pressed and released quickly, the state of the sensor is Bumped. The release must occur within 0.5 seconds to be considered Bumped.

In a Wait block or at the start of a Switch block are good points in your program to place code that uses the Touch sensor. Choose Pressed if you want the block to be triggered at the instant the Touch sensor is pressed. Choose Released if you want the block to be triggered at the instant the Touch sensor is released.

Both the LEGO MINDSTORMS Education NXT Base Set (9797) and the LEGO MINDSTORMS 2.0 retail set include two NXT Touch sensors. Currently, FLL rules allow for multiple Touch sensors. But check the rules each year since they are subject to change. Also, there are companies that make a Touch Sensor Multiplexer that lets you have up to four Touch sensors on one NXT sensor port, but these multiplexers are not allowed in FLL events.

Using the Touch Sensor

Unlike the Light sensor, the Touch sensor does not need any special calibration to perform its job. It only returns the value of the current state of the sensor—pressed or released. Figure 9-3 shows the sensor being pressed. The mechanism is a simple switch—no calibration is needed.

Figure 9-3. Pressing the Touch sensor

When Is Pressed Not Pressed?

When using the Touch sensor, you must be certain that the button is activated the way you want it to be. If the sensor is not square with the object to be pressed, it may register as Bumped—just a glancing blow. Also, if the robot bounces off an object quickly, the Touch sensor may only register it as Bumped (if it registers at all). It is important to make sure that when you want the Touch sensor pressed, it is squarely pressed and remains pressed.

Determining When to Turn

One purpose of the Touch sensor is to know when the robot has reached an obstacle in its path. It functions as a feeler or bumper for your robot. You can place an axle in the Touch sensor's axle hole, and depending on the design of your robot, the axle will let the robot know when to turn to avoid an obstacle. Determining the length of the axle is important. You must take into consideration several factors. One is the placement of the Touch sensor. If the sensor is located at the rear of the robot, the axle may not be long enough to reach the obstacle before the front of the robot runs into it, as depicted in Figure 9-4.

Figure 9-4. The Touch sensor may not reach the obstacle in time

Likewise, placing the sensor's axle probe too close to the obstacle will not leave enough distance to navigate around other obstacles, as seen in Figure 9-5.

Figure 9-5. The Touch sensor is too close to the obstacle

Therefore, in developing your program to solve a mission using the Touch sensor, it is important that you take note of several factors:

- **The overall design of the robot.** What does your wheelbase look like? What is its turning radius? Which attachments must you be aware of? Where will the Touch sensor be placed?

- **The obstacles that are in your way.** How tall or short are the obstacles? What happens if you miss touching an obstacle?

- **What happens next.** Is there more than one direction to turn after touching an obstacle? How do you determine which direction to turn? Do you have enough room to maneuver the robot around an obstacle, or are other obstacles in the way (e.g., a maze)?

Squaring Up

You can use the border walls in a challenge to square your robot and help ensure its position relative to the playing field. Use the lines as described in Chapter 8 to get your bearings on the table. Then use the table borders to square your robot to a mission. Applying both techniques will enable you to consistently score points in a challenge.

Just as you need two Light sensors to align a robot to a line on the playing field, you also need two Touch sensors to align a robot to a border wall. Figure 9-6 shows a common configuration.

Figure 9-6. A robot with two Touch sensors

COMPUTER SCIENCE EXAMPLE

One of the ways to use Touch sensors to square the robot is to mount them so that they are aimed backward, placed parallel to each other and the direction of the robot. Programming the robot then introduces you to the term *finite-state machine*.

A State machine is any device that stores the status of something at a given time and can operate on input to change the status of and/or cause an action or output for any given change. A finite-state machine is one that has a limited or finite number of possible states[1].

Imagine a device that reads a long sheet of paper, for example. There is a single letter—a or b—printed on every inch of the paper. As the State machine reads each letter, it changes its state, as shown in the following.

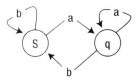

A State machine example

The circles represent "states" that the machine can be in. The arrows are the transitions to determine which state to go to next. For example, if you are in state "s" and read an "a", you'll transition to state "q". If you read a "b", you'll stay in state "s".

We can use the finite-state machine to show how we can code the squaring of the robot using two Touch sensors. The following figure is a state transition diagram for driving with two Touch sensors. There are three possibilities coming from each state.

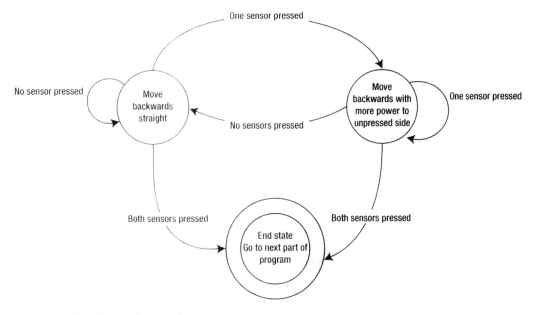

A State machine diagram for squaring

You don't *need* to be aware of terms like "finite-state machine" in order to square your robot. However, you'll gain deeper understanding from knowing this bit of theory. You'll make a better impression on the judges, too.

---

[1]For more on State machines, see http://blog.markwshead.com/869/state-machines-computer-science and http://searchcio-midmarket.techtarget.com/definition/state-machine.

In NXT-G, one way to square your robot using Touch sensors is by using code that just keeps driving backward until both Touch sensors are pressed. Before ending the loop, the logic loop tests to make sure that both Touch sensor #1 *and* Touch sensor #2 are pressed. It then stops the motors. The example shown in Figure 9-7 is the code snippet from within a MyBlock called SquareUp1.

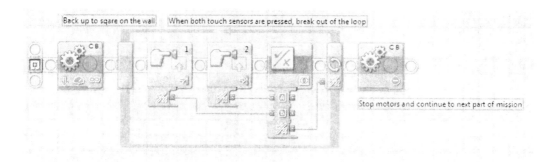

Figure 9-7. *A program to square the robot by driving backward until both Touch sensors are pressed*

This MyBlock is effective as long as the robot starts the SquareUp1 routine relatively square to the wall. If the robot is not square, then you can use another program that moves the wheels backward independently, as described in our State machine example. Figure 9-8 shows another way to write a MyBlock (SquareUp2) for squaring the robot.

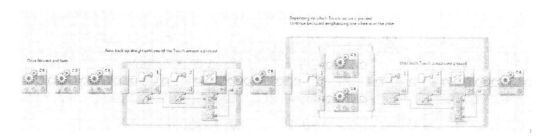

Figure 9-8. *An alternate method for squaring the robot*

Remote NXT Orange Button

During FLL competitions, you only have 2.5 minutes to solve as many missions as you can. You want to use every second to score as high as possible. If you spend the first three to five seconds fumbling with the orange and gray buttons on top of the NXT, you're wasting precious time. The Touch sensor can come to your rescue. At the start of a run, you have a short amount of time to set up the robot, get your attachments in order, and prepare for the "3-2-1 LEGO!" start. You can use the Touch sensor as the starting point for your missions by using the code snippet in Figure 9-9 (another candidate for a MyBlock).

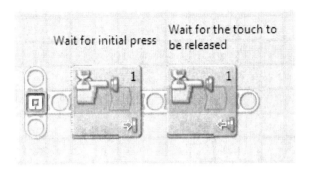

Figure 9-9. Wait for the touch release to start the program

Placing a MyBlock that contains Figure 9-9's code at the start of your mission programs lets you start each program running—without moving. You can align your robot at the start of the clock, and when ready, let the referees know that it's okay to start the match. You simply press and hold the Touch sensor until you are ready to send the robot on its way. When you release the Touch sensor, the robot will start moving.

Limit Switch

One thing about NXT-G is that code blocks will run to completion. This can be a blessing as well as a curse. As you debug your programs, for example, it is helpful to know that a Move block will continue executing until it has reached its end state (e.g., three rotations) and moves to the next block. However, if you are moving an arm or another manipulator to a certain location and something gets in its way, the program will wait for the Move block to complete its rotations before moving on. Of course, something is in the way, so the movement will never complete—making it appear as if the program is stuck or broken. Yet during your robot design, you can incorporate a Touch sensor to act as a Limit switch or an indicator that the robot's arm has reached its desired location. Such an approach has advantages over simply waiting for a given number of rotations.

A *Limit switch* is a sensor that prevents the travel of a mechanism beyond a predetermined point. The switch is mechanically operated by the motion of the mechanism itself. In the following example, the robot is going to lower an arm to pick up an object. If you use rotations to lower the arm but you don't have the arm in the right location to start, then the arm may come down short of your desired location. Or the arm could go too far down, and thus never complete the rotations as it gets stuck pounding against the table.

Using the Touch sensor as a Limit switch ensures that you hit the desired spot to pick up an object every time. Design your robot with the Touch sensor on the arm. Figure 9-10 shows a program that makes use of the Touch sensor as a Limit switch. Move the arm with unlimited duration until the Limit switch (Touch sensor) is pressed. Pick up the target object and raise the arm. You can probably get away with raising the arm any number of rotations on the motor. You can then return your robot to base.

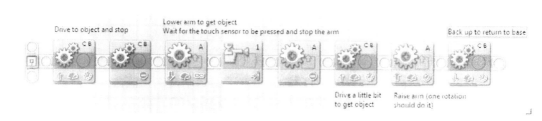

Figure 9-10. *Use of a Touch sensor as a Limit switch*

Another way to return the arm to the starting position is to add a calculation to return the mechanism the same number of rotations that you used to originally move it. You do this using the built-in rotation sensor on the motor driving the mechanism, as shown in Figure 9-11.

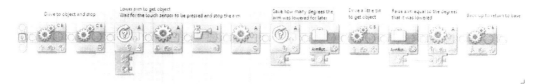

Figure 9-11. *Another Limit switch example returns the arm to starting location*

Touch Sensor As an Indicator of an Object

Another way to use the Touch sensor is to determine whether you've placed an object on your robot. It works similar to placing food on a grocery scale. Place a Touch sensor underneath a platform resting on top of the sensor. When you place something on the platform, the Touch sensor is Pressed.

Summary

Although it is one of the simplest sensors to use, the Touch sensor is also one of the most powerful sensors in your robot toolbox. A full understanding of the Touch sensor—including detecting when it is Pressed or Released—is critical to its proper use in competitions.

Chapter 10

Seeing with Ultrasonics

The LEGO MINDSTORMS Ultrasonic sensor is another way to give your robot the gift of sight. Unlike the Light sensor, which detects reflected light, the Ultrasonic sensor works by sending out a sonic wave that reflects off objects in front of the sensor. The wave reflects back to the sensor, which determines its distance from the object based on the amount of time it took the sonic wave to return. This is similar to the way that animals such as bats see at night.

The sonic wave has a much longer range of detection than the Light sensor. But you need to be careful with the way you use the Ultrasonic sensor at robot events. Various factors affect how the sensor detects objects in its environment.

How It Works

Figure 10-1 shows the Configuration panel for the Ultrasonic sensor block. The panel settings are similar to the other sensors in that you need to select the port that the Ultrasonic sensor is connected to. Then you select the distance you wish to use for a comparison. You do this either with the slide bar or by typing in the value directly.

Note The sensor can measure an object up to 100 inches (250 centimeters) away from the sensor.

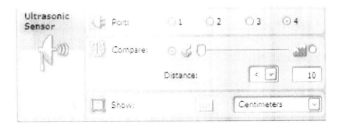

Figure 10-1. *Ultrasonic sensor Control panel settings*

You also set the trigger to look for distances either less than or greater than the distance you have entered. The Show property allows you to select either inches or centimeters. When working with objects that are close to the sensor, centimeters will give better accuracy.

A simple program to write for the Ultrasonic sensor is one that displays the distance to an object. The idea is to show the current reading of the sensor on the screen of the NXT. You can use the program as a fancy measuring tape.

Figure 10-2 shows an example of such a program. Inside the control loop, an Ultrasonic sensor block passes the distance value to a Number to Text block. The converted value is then passed to the Display block. The value will be shown in either inches or centimeters on the Ultrasonic sensor block.

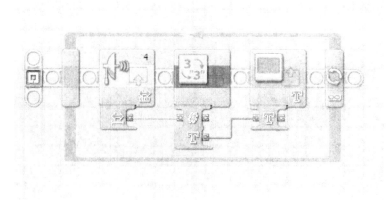

Figure 10-2. *A digital tape measure program using the Ultrasonic sensor*

Making It Work on the Game Field

The NXT Ultrasonic sensor can be very helpful in detecting large objects on the game field. The sensor should always be mounted in a horizontal position for accurate readings. Again, centimeters work better than inches when trying to detect close objects. Distances less than 3 millimeters cannot be read accurately by the sensor. Accuracy is decreased when objects are further than 25 centimeters from the sensor. The optimum range for the Ultrasonic sensor is between 3 centimeters and 25 centimeters. The receiver is located on the left side of the sensor, making the sensor stronger at detecting objects on the right side of it, where the sonic signal is transmitted.

The View tools built into the NXT brick are very helpful in calculating the distance of objects and the proper placement of the Ultrasonic sensor on your robot. Experiment with various locations to see which position gives you the most consistent measurement for detecting a particular object on the field.

When using the Ultrasonic sensor in a competition where other robots are running close by, it is a good idea to keep the sensor mounted lower than the walls on the game table. There is the possibility that another robot is also using an Ultrasonic sensor Your robot's sensor can become confused if another robot's sonic signals are detected. By keeping your sensor lower than the table walls, you will minimize the risk of confusion.

The Ultrasonic sensor works very well at detecting large, flat objects that are approximately perpendicular to the line between the sensor and the object. Objects that are smaller or rounded may not be accurately detected. In the 2009 FLL Smart Moves games, there were a series of "sensor walls" that the robots had to detect and either knock down or navigate around. If your strategy were to avoid the walls, then a Bumper or Touch sensor was not an ideal way to detect them. The Ultrasonic sensor was perfect for this task since the walls were rather large and flat; it had little trouble detecting them. Figure 10-3 illustrates a robot with an Ultrasonic sensor installed on its front. It is trying to detect a LEGO wall field object.

Figure 10-3. A robot with an Ultrasonic sensor that is detecting a sensor wall

Beware of unintended objects getting in the Ultrasonic sensor's view path. During competitions, for example, referees or team members may have to reach onto the game field to remove a stray object, during which time their hands could get in the path of a robot's sensor. Be careful not to allow your robot to detect a person reaching onto the field. Otherwise, thinking that it has encountered an obstacle, your robot could change its course.

Finding Nearby Objects

A simple task for the Ultrasonic sensor is to search for objects or obstacles in the area. Let's say you're participating in a LEGO Sumo Bot game in which two robots on a game field try to push each other out of bounds. Most of the time, these games are held on a circular black field with a white edge bordering the area. The robots start the game side by side in the middle of the field. The robots wait five seconds before trying to push each other out of the field. Figure 10-4 shows a simple Sumo Bot practice game.

Figure 10-4. A team practicing their Sumo Bots on the game field

You could simply have your robot travel randomly inside the boundary until it runs into the other robot, and then try to push the other robot out of bounds. With a Light sensor, your robot could detect the edge of the field and change direction when it finds the edge. The diagram in Figure 10-5 maps out this concept.

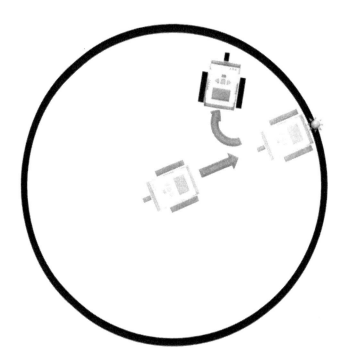

Figure 10-5. The robot starts in the middle, moves forward to detect the edge with a Light sensor, and backs up and turns when the edge is detected

This strategy will only get you so far before a smarter robot takes you out, but the program looks something like Figure 10-6.

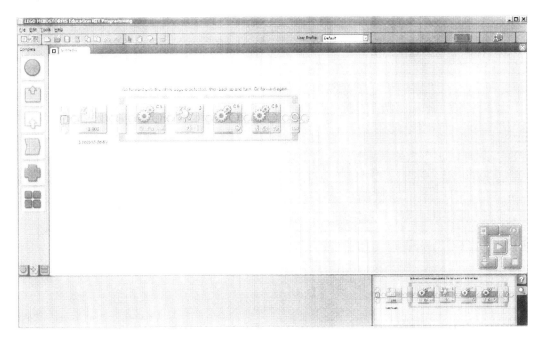

Figure 10-6. A simple Sumo Bot program with edge detection

The smart approach would be for your robot to scan the game field for the other robot, and once it is located, try to push it out of limits, as shown in Figure 10-7.

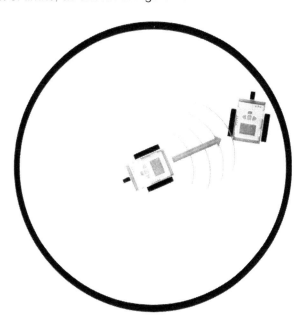

Figure 10-7. The robot will scan with the Ultrasonic sensor, and once it finds the other robot, move forward to make contact

Take a look at the Wait block using the Ultrasonic sensor as the sensor type in Figure 10-8. The Until parameter uses Distance and waits until an object is detected within the given distance.

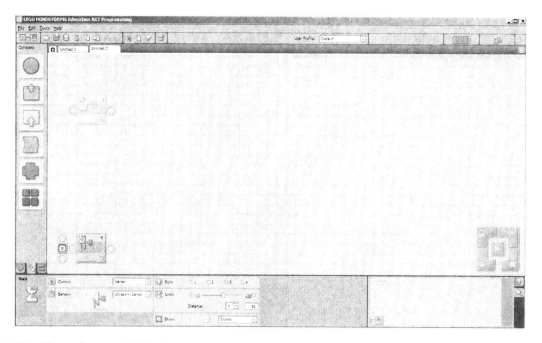

Figure 10-8. Ultrasonic sensor Wait block

Incorporating the Wait block with the Ultrasonic sensor for our sumo robot program is a simple process. If your robot is in scan mode, it simply sits in the middle of the game field and rotates 360 degrees until the Wait block detects the other robot within the given distance, as seen in Figure 10-9.

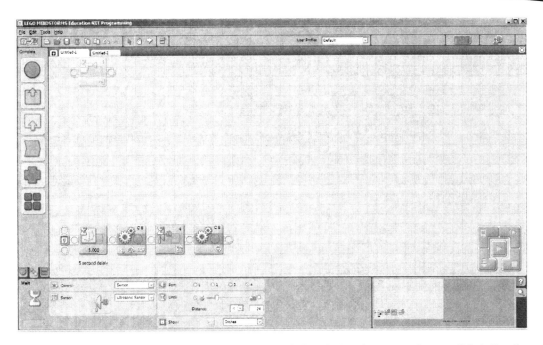

Figure 10-9. *The robot turns in a circle looking for the other robot within 24 inches. It stops rotating once it finds the other robot*

Once the Ultrasonic sensor detects the other robot, the Move blocks stops and the robot will move in the direction of the other robot (see Figure 10-10).

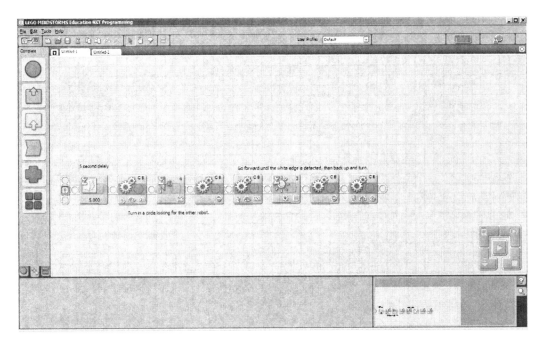

Figure 10-10. *Now the robot moves forward as before, hoping to push the other robot while still seeking the edge of the table so that it doesn't drive itself off the game field*

Now you just need to wrap this program in a loop and you will have a simple Sumo Bot program (see Figure 10-11). Be sure to give the robot plenty of room to spin around when it finds the edge of the table. Back up a good distance from the table edge, or else your robot could put itself out of the event by driving off the sumo game table.

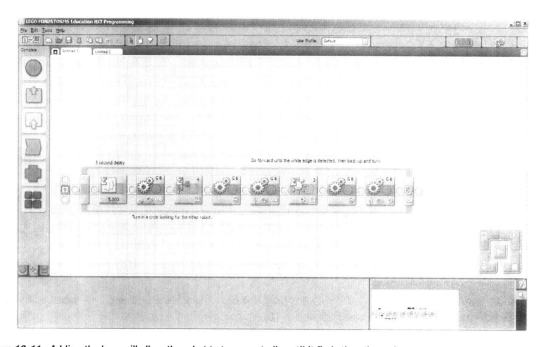

Figure 10-11. Adding the loop will allow the robot to try repeatedly until it finds the other robot

If you really wanted to get fancy, your robot could use multiple Ultrasonic sensors. The MINDSTORMS NXT has four sensor inputs, so you can actually connect three Ultrasonic sensors to the robot—on the front, right, and left sides—and a Light sensor on port 4. This would allow your robot to sit and wait for one of the three sensors to detect the location of the opposing robot. Note that the LEGO MINDSTORMS kit only includes a single Ultrasonic sensor, so the other sensors would have to be purchased separately.

The sensors feed into a Switch block. The direction your robot positions itself to move forward and make contact with the opposing robot is determined by the Ultrasonic sensor that detects the other robot. The flow diagram in Figure 10-12 maps out the logic for making this work.

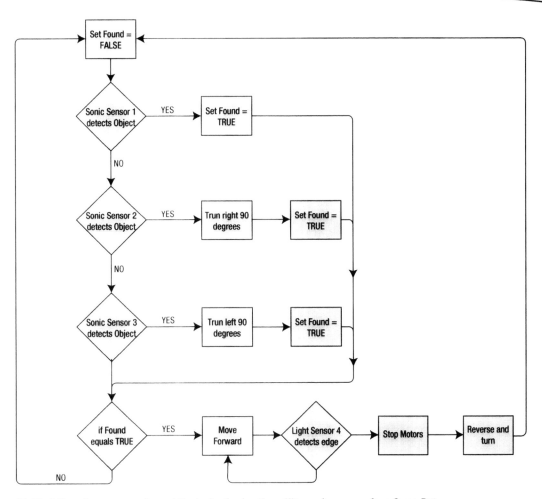

Figure 10-12. A flow diagram mapping out the logic of using three Ultrasonic sensors for a Sumo Bot

Figure 10-13 shows the NXT-G code for making use of three Ultrasonic sensors. Don't worry if you cannot read the details. You can download the code from the Apress web site (www.apress.com) to view the code in more detail.

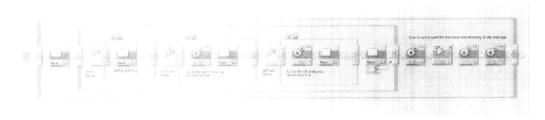

Figure 10-13. A Sumo Bot program using three Ultrasonic sensors

Summary

Even though the Ultrasonic sensor is not one of the more popular sensors used in LEGO robotic events, it can be a very powerful tool. If used properly, it gives your robot the ability to detect and sense obstacles without having to make direct contact. This is not only effective in avoiding things, but at the same time it allows your robot to make decisions from a distance—saving you time that can be put to better use in accomplishing your goals.

Technical judges will be looking for teams that take advantage of all the sensors available, as long as using the sensor makes sense. Be sure that your team can explain not only why you are using an Ultrasonic sensor, but also make sure you understand how and why it works.

Chapter 11

Programming Like a Pro

The basics of writing a good NXT-G program were covered in the previous chapters. Most of the techniques that we discussed are all that a team would ever need to know to compete in a LEGO robotic event. But there may be times when your team wants to go beyond the "normal" and add something extra to your code. You may want to create a robot that can store information about the game field in an array for future use, or you may want to create a master program, also called a *sequencer*, to help your team switch between programs more quickly at an event.

Introducing more complex coding to your robot can add nice talking points when presenting your robot's programs to technical judges. Be careful though. Don't add unnecessary complexity just for the sake of making your programs complicated; doing so won't impress the judges. But if you can effectively demonstrate why you wrote the code, and explain it proficiently, then the judges will enjoy seeing your more sophisticated programs.

Data Arrays

An array is a collection of data normally referenced by an index value. To access the different values in an array, you reference the array definition and give it an index of the value you wish to read or write to. The concept is very common in most programming languages but not in NXT-G, so when there is the need for an array, you will have to simulate an array with a series of Variable blocks and a Switch block.

You may have a mission on your game field that requires the robot to act differently based on some field conditions, such as finding a ball and performing a particular action based on the color of that ball. In your array, you could store the actions needed based on the ball color. The ball color would become your array index and the action would be the value.

The example in Figure 11-1 shows a very simple ReadArray MyBlock that has four index values and contains a Text data type. For the code to work, there has to be four text Variables defined. If you need more values, then you will have to expand your Switch block and define extra Variable blocks as well.

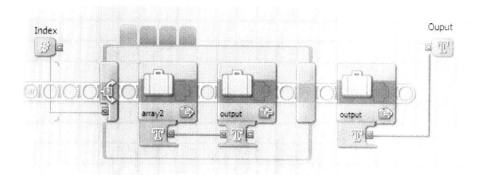

Figure 11-1. *Reading text values from a series of Variable blocks being used as an array by having a Switch block return values based on the index value*

When used as shown in Figure 11-2, you simply pass in the index value of the data you wish to read and it is returned as the output of the My Block.

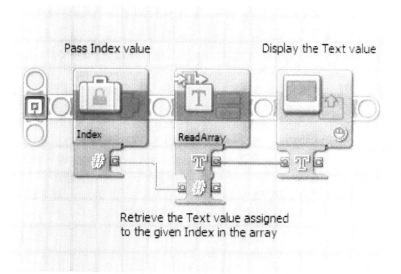

Figure 11-2. *The ReadArray My Block used to display values on the NXT display screen based on the index value given*

The concept would be very much the same for a WriteArray My Block. You would simply change the direction of the input and output values, as shown in Figure 11-3.

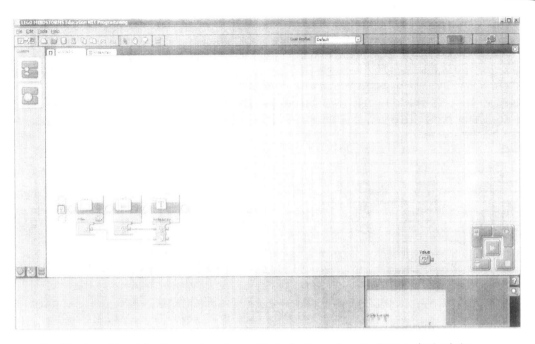

Figure 11-3. *The WriteArray block takes in an index value and the text value assigned to the array in that index*

State Machines

With NXT-G, the ability to perform *preemptive multitasking* is desirable for a robot navigating a game field. Preemptive multitasking allows a robot to suspend one task while it focuses on another, and then return to the first task. For example, a robot might encounter an obstacle while navigating across the game field. You'll want the robot to navigate around the obstacle, and then return to its primary task of moving to your target destination.

Preemptive multitasking isn't built into the NXT-G language. But you can approximate it through the creative use of Switch blocks.

Let's say your robot is on a mission to seek out and collect an object on the game field, but there is the possibility of an obstacle in the path. Furthermore, at the time you start the program, you do not know whether the obstacle is present. Thus, your robot must make a decision based on its sensor readings. Figure 11-4 illustrates a normal sequence—assuming there is nothing in the way of the robot.

Figure 11-4. *A simple program to allow the robot to move forward 8 inches and then turn right and travel 3 inches*

What if your logic needs to change—or change "state"? How can you interrupt the current sequence? Here you take advantage of the Move block; one sequence beam can start a Move action while a second sequence beam can stop the Move block, thus giving you the ability to change state. A variable is added to keep track of the state the robot is currently in. To keep things simple, our example will only have four states: (1) move forward, (2) turn right, (3) turn left, and (4) stop. The Switch block in Figure 11-5 will decide which action needs to be taken, depending on the current value in the state Variable block. The state Variable block will also have the next state value set for the sequence.

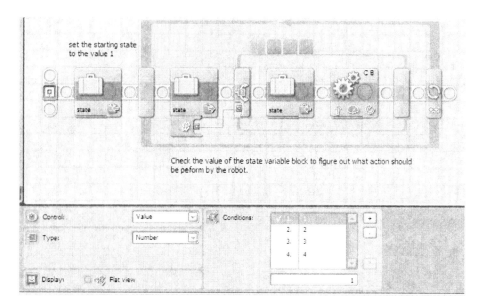

Figure 11-5. *A Switch block to control the actions of each state value. A value of (1) move forward, (2) turn right, (3) turn left, and (4) stop. The value starts out as a 1 to move forward and then cycles through each of the states*

By adding a second sequence beam, the program can keep an eye out for obstacles in the path and change the state accordingly. In this example, the robot needs to turn left if it encounters anything in its way (state value = 3). In Figure 11-6, the logic is that if the Ultrasonic sensor detects an object, the robot stops its current task and changes its state to turn left. This is done by stopping the Move block and then setting the state Variable block to a value of 3.

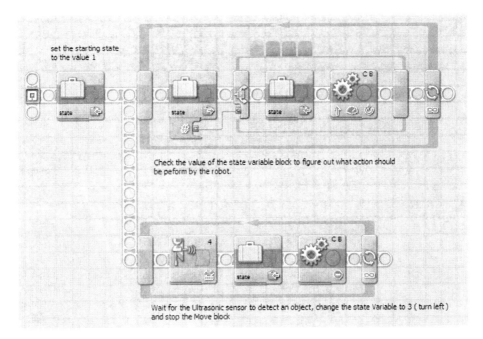

set the starting state to the value 1

Check the value of the state variable block to figure out what action should be peform by the robot.

Wait for the Ultrasonic sensor to detect an object, change the state Variable to 3 (turn left) and stop the Move block

Figure 11-6. A second sequence beam to check the Ultrasonic sensor and change the robot's state to 3 (turn left) if an obstacle is found

Master Programs

A winning robot is more than just a fancy robot chassis with some cool attachments. Your robot's programs are essential to having a robot that performs well at a competition. Most teams develop a collection of programs to complete their missions. One of the biggest uses of time during a LEGO robotics event is the switching between each of these programs as the robot completes a mission. Even though the LEGO NXT brick provides a nice interface for switching between programs, it can be time-consuming to search through the list of programs and select the right one for the next mission.

To speed things up, the process of selecting the necessary program can be done with a master program, or sequencer. The concept is that you write each of the missions' programs as subprograms, or My Blocks as they're called in NXT-G. Then write a master program that will call each of the subprograms in the required order.

A simple master program cycles through the programs one after another. When each of the programs completes or a particular event has occurred—such as a pressed Touch sensor or other sensor event—then you can go to the other extreme and have a master program that not only advances automatically, but allows the user to navigate the list of programs and run a program out of order if needed. This idea builds upon data arrays—the subprograms are the values in the array sequenced by the State machine. Master programs can be simple or complicated—it just depends on what your team needs and wants to do.

I recommend having some form of a master program to help speed up the process for program selection; this can be a key factor in saving valuable time at an event. Also, having a master program can be one of the important programming items that judges look for during technical reviews. If you have developed a master program, be sure to point this out to your technical judges and be ready to explain how it works and why you have it.

My Blocks

For a master program to work, each of your mission programs needs to be saved as NXT-G My Blocks. My Blocks are really subprograms that can be accessed by other NXT-G programs. Don't worry about turning your mission programs into My Blocks until you have the mission programs working as you desire. It's much easier to debug and test the programs when they are still NXT-G programs. But even after a program is converted to a My Block, you are able to run it as an individual program for testing and debugging.

When writing your mission programs for a master program, it is important that they each have a defined start event and end event. The start event is simply the first action in the program—so that part is easy and already done. But a defined end is not always so easy. Many times, teams have their robot drive an unlimited amount of time and merely depend on a team remember to grab the robot when it crosses the base line and stop the program with the controls on the NXT.

You won't have success when manual intervention is required. You do not want to press the Stop button on the NXT brick because doing so will actually stop your master program and not just the My Block that you're currently running. Instead, your program should end with an event from a sensor or end when a particular duration is met, such as a particular number of motor rotations. This way, your program is not depending on someone to press the Stop button on the NXT brick to end the program's execution.

A Touch sensor can be added to your robot so that once it is pressed, the program knows to stop. Figure 11-7 is an NXT-G program that runs a series of missions and then returns to base. Once the wall is detected, the program will know it has reached base and allow the program to stop. A program such as this makes a nice My Block.

Figure 11-7. NXT-G sample mission code

As noted in Chapter 3, adding a Motor Reset block to the beginning of each subprogram prevents the My Blocks from causing calculation issues with the NXT-G software tracking the rotations. Many times when you switch from various subprograms that all have code that relies on rotation calculations, the actual number of rotations can get out of sync—but again, the Motor Reset block can prevent this from happening.

Simple Sequencer Program

The most common and easy-to-write master program is a simple sequence program. This master program will run the subprograms in a preprogrammed order. For most teams, this is a good start and meets the needs of the team. The drawbacks of such a program are when something has to change on the fly. Say, for example, you need to rerun a subprogram. If the master program has no way to navigate through the programs, then the user is forced to exit the master program and search for the subprogram using the standard NXT file menu system—thus costing valuable time.

Even though a simple master program has limitations, it's a good place to start. Once the team has a good grasp of the purpose of such a program, they can continue to build onto it and add new features such as program navigation, display options, and program state memory. These concepts will be covered when advanced master programs are discussed later in the chapter.

The Scenario

A robot game that has a series of nine missions that the robot must complete in 2.5 minutes is a situation in which a master program is necessary. In our example, the team has written five programs that will complete all the missions. This means some of the programs will handle more than one mission. This is always a good thing and the first step in saving time. Whenever a team can combine missions into a single program, it is a more efficient use of time and resources.

The team has five programs that they will run in the same order each time they compete. The following is a list of the example programs that the team wants to run:

1.   Collect Scientist Minifigs

2.   Gather Core Sample and Stray Ball

3.   Deliver Simple Machine and Scientist Minifigs

4.   Deliver Car and Pallet of Power

5.   Go to Final Parking Place and Deliver Package

Note   When naming your programs, it's always a good idea to give them a name that describes what the program does. Names like Program1 or MyProgram don't give the user an idea of what the program will actually do.

Looking at the program names in the list, you see that some of the programs have to be run in a particular order. For example, the program called "Collect Scientist Minifigs" needs to run before "Deliver Simple Machine and Scientist Minifigs" since we must first collect the Scientist Minifigs before we can deliver them. Other programs might not be dependent on previous programs, so their order is not as important. What is important is that you come up with an order and then practice running the robot in that order repeatedly. With each of these programs, the robot returns to base when completed. Any new attachments are then added and the next program is selected so that the robot can venture out again and attempt to complete the missions.

If you have worked with the NXT file menu system, you have learned that the NXT puts the loaded programs in FILO order (first in, last out). So as you load your programs into the NXT brick, the very first program you load will always be the very last program in the sequence as you navigate through the list of programs with the NXT file system navigation tools.

It is very time-consuming to flip through the programs each time the robot returns to base just to find the next program in your desired sequence. A simple sequencer program will resolve this issue and help the team quickly move forward during a competition.

Creating My Blocks

One of the first things the team will need to do in our example is convert each of their programs into NXT-G My Blocks. To do this, make sure each program has a defined end point, as we discussed earlier. None of the programs should depend on the user pressing the Stop button on the NXT brick since this will not only stop the My Block program but will stop our master program as well.

To convert our programs into My Blocks, we simply select each program on the NXT-G programming screen. Make sure all the blocks and wires are selected. We don't want to leave anything out. Then from the Edit menu, select Make a New My Block. Give your new My Block a name that will allow the user to understand what the My Block does without having to study the code. Ideally, a user should be able to read the name of the My Block to understand what the program does. My Blocks also allow the user to enter a brief description of the My Block. It is a good place for other users to better understand the code.

Creating the Sequencer

So now that we have the My Blocks for each of the programs created and we know the order we want to run them, we are ready to create a simple sequencer program to run the programs in order. In our NXT-G code, we will need a counter to keep track of where we are in the sequence of programs, and a Switch block to switch between each of the programs. Think about the State machine that you read about earlier in this chapter; this is the same concept. We will use the orange button on the top of the NXT brick as our trigger for switching between the programs. Every time the robot returns to base, one of the team members will simply press the orange button, increasing the counter in our master program by one. The Switch block will use the value of the counter to know which My Block to run next. This is much faster than a team member navigating the NXT file system to find the next desired program. It also eliminates the possibility of the user selecting the wrong program.

Looking at the Code

Let's look at the code in Figure 11-8 in detail. At the start of our code, we set the counter to the value of 0. Even though we have five programs, they will be represented by the counter values 0 through 4. Since we are using a loop to rotate through the programs, we could use the counter value that is included with the Loop block, but as we build on the program, the Counter variable will become more useful.

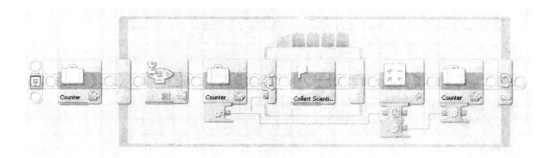

Figure 11-8. A simple sequencer master program

Once we enter the Loop block, the program stops at a Wait block until the orange button on the NXT brick is pressed. When this happens, the code moves to the Switch block. The Switch block is connected to our Counter variable, which executes whatever My Block we have associated with the counter sequence. Figure 11-5 shows that the My Block "Collect Scientist Minifigs" is the first tab on the Switch block. When the My Block in the Switch block is executed to completion, the Counter variable is incremented by 1 using the Math block. The new value is saved back into the Counter variable.

This program works as a master program in the simplest form. What can we do to improve it? First, it needs is some form of feedback that notifies the user which program is currently running. It also needs some kind of indication that the user has pressed the orange button. It is important that the user have feedback so that he knows what the robot is attempting to do next.

Figure 11-9 shows that a Sound block has been added after the Wait block so that when the orange button is pressed, a tone will sound to let the user know that the button press was received by the program. Before the Wait block, a Number to Text block was added to convert the value of the Counter to a text value so that it can be displayed on the NXT screen. This allows the users to know where they are in the sequence process.

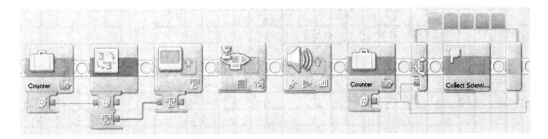

Figure 11-9. A simple sequencer with feedback such as tones and displays

Better Sequencer

As you saw with our Simple Sequencer master program, the concept is very straightforward: run the program and then wait for the user to tell the master program to run the next program in the correct order. This is a big time-saver when trying to run a series of programs at a robotics competition. But what happens if you need to change things at the last minute? What if you need to rerun the same program before advancing to the next program?

Take the first program, Collect Scientist Minifigs, for example. Perhaps the robot missed collecting the minifigs and you need them for the second mission. You know if you run the program again, you might have a chance at collecting them, but your Simple Sequencer program has already advanced to the next program in your list. This is a case in which having advanced features such as program navigation in your program is helpful.

Program Navigation

If we look at the code used for the Simple Sequencer master program, you see that the Counter variable is the value controlling which program is running. So if there was a way to change the value of the Counter variable in either forward or backward directions, we would have more control over which programs are run in what sequence. If we want to rerun the Collect Scientist Minifigs program, all we need to do is get the value of the Counter variable back to 0 since this program is the first in our sequence. In Figure 11-10, there is a new thread that has a Wait block. This Wait block is waiting for the Left Arrow button in the NXT brick to be bumped. Using Bumped instead of Pressed is important, because if we used Pressed, the value would decrement continuously until the button was released. When the left arrow is bumped, the value of the Counter variable is decremented by 1. In our example, this would put us back at 0, which is where we want to be to rerun the first program in our sequence.

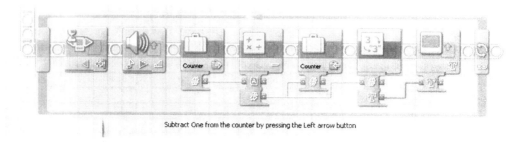

Subtract One from the counter by pressing the Left arrow button

Figure 11-10. NXT-G code to navigate to previous programs in the sequence

There is also a new Display block and Number to Text block added so that the user can see which program in the sequence is next. If we build on this concept, we can add a third thread for the Right Arrow button to allow the user to increment the Counter variable and move forward in the sequence of programs. This would be useful if one of the programs needed to be skipped, for example. Figure 11-11 shows the addition of the third thread to include the Right Arrow button bump event.

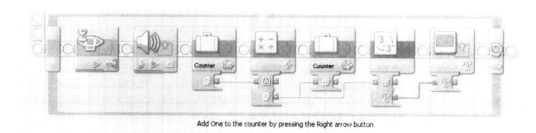

Add One to the counter by pressing the Right arrow button

Figure 11-11. Navigation code to skip forward in the sequence

Sequence Rollover

You might have noticed from the previous code samples that it wouldn't take long before our Counter variable exceeds the number of programs in our sequence or goes to a negative number. It would be wise to add some code to prevent the Counter value from going below 0 or from going higher than the number of programs we will actually need to run in our sequencer.

We can add a new My Block to our code that will handle the math for us and not allow the value to go out of range. In our example, the sequence range is 0 through 4. We are currently using Math blocks to increment or decrement our Counter value. So all we need to do is create a new My Block called SequenceMath block. The code would look like Figure 11-12.

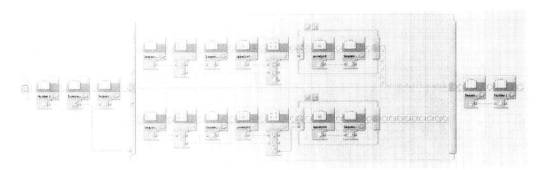

Figure 11-12. A NXT-G program to cause the sequence counter to roll over if it falls out of range

The logic for this new program is as follows:

1. Input the current sequence value.

2. Determine whether we are incrementing or decrementing the sequence value (True/False).

3. Assign the current sequence value to the Sequence variable.

4. If we are incrementing, then follow the True branch; otherwise, follow the False branch.

5. In the True branch, add 1 to the Sequence variable.

6. Check if the Sequence variable value is greater than the UpperLimit constant (a value of 4 in our example).

7. If the Sequence value is greater than the UpperLimit, assign the LowerLimit to the value of the Sequence.

8. In the False branch, subtract 1 from the Sequence variable.

9. Check if the Sequence variable is less than the LowerLimit constant (a value of 0 in our example).

10. If the Sequence value is less than the LowerLimit, assign the UpperLimit to the value of the Sequence.

11. Output the Sequence variable value.

Follow the code in Figure 11-13 from the beginning. You'll see that two input values are accepted: a number variable called Number 1 and a Logic variable called Increment. The Number 1 variable will be the current value of our Counter variable, and that value is saved in the SequenceNumber variable. The Increment variable tells the program if we want to increase or decrease the value of our SequenceNumber. The reason we assign the Number 1 variable to the Sequence variable is so that when we make it into a My Block, the Number 1 variable and the Increment variable will become input parameters for our new block.

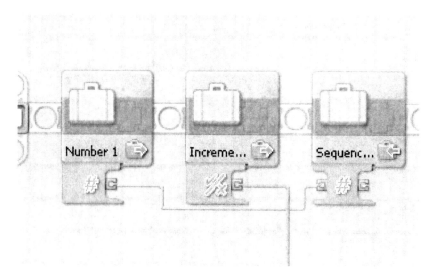

Figure 11-13. Setting up the input parameters

The Increment variable value is now passed to a Switch block in Figure 11-14. The True path will add 1 to the SequenceNumber value and the False path will subtract 1 from the SequenceNumber value.

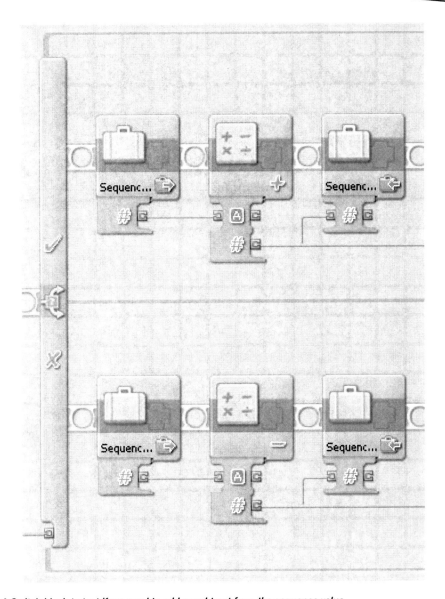

Figure 11-14. A Switch block to test if we need to add or subtract from the sequence value

After it has done the math on the SequenceNumber value, another Switch block will follow to see if you have exceeded our defined range of programs, as seen in Figure 11-15. This program has two constants defined: UpperLimit and LowerLimit. The UpperLimit is defined as 4 for our example and the LowerLimit is defined as 0. Remember, the range for our example is 0 through 4.

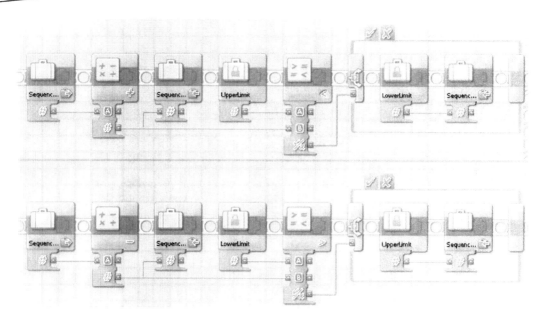

Figure 11-15. Checking the new value of the Sequence variable to see if it's out of range of our upper and lower limits

If the Switch block finds that we have either exceeded the defined range or fallen under the range value, then it will simply reassign the SequenceNumber to the inverse limit value. For example, if our current SequenceNumber is 4 and then we add 1 to it, our SequenceNumber is now equal to 5. The value of 5 is outside the desired range, so we set the SequenceNumber to the LowerLimit of our range, 0. Now the SequenceNumber becomes 0. The opposite is true as well: if the SequenceNumber falls below the LowerLimit, the SequenceNumber will be reset to the UpperLimit of 4.

Now convert the program into a My Block called SequenceMath. The new My Block has two input parameters: Increment (True/False) and the Sequence In (Integer). There is also one output parameter named Sequence Out. The input parameters are seen in Figure 11-16.

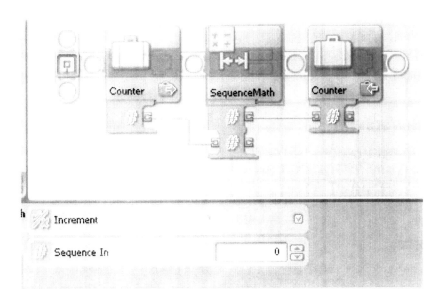

Figure 11-16. *The SequenceMath My Block that was created from the code*

Now we can replace the Math block in our current program with the new SequenceMath block. This will keep our program from placing our sequencer out of range. If the range changes for our programs, then all that you need to do is adjust the UpperLimit constant in the SequenceMath block. Figure 11-17 shows the revised master program with these changes in place.

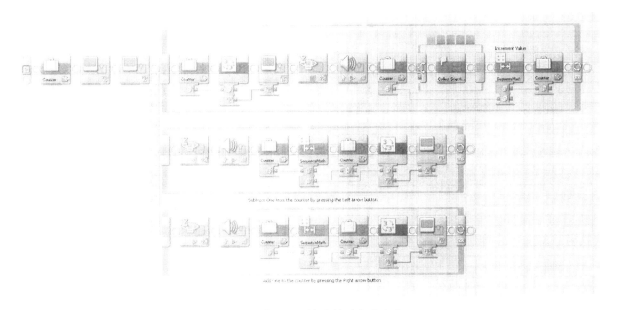

Figure 11-17. *Revised master program with the new SequenceMath block included*

You may find that you don't want the sequence to roll over when you get to the upper limit of your range. You may prefer that it just simply stop incrementing. To prevent incrementing beyond the limit, you simply assign the value of the UpperLimit constant to your sequence when you reach the limit. That way, any attempt to exceed the limit causes the limit to be reassigned to the variable.

Advanced Sequencer

The previous two versions of the sequencer will make great starting points for master programs. With very little effort, your team should be able to quickly add some nice user messages to the interface and perform well at any robotics event. If you want to add a little extra to your program, you could do something even more advanced.

Program Display

Thus far, the master program, Better Sequencer, displays the program sequence number on the NXT screen. This is great if you have memorized the order of your programs and know that when you see 0 on the screen, it refers to the My Block named Collect Scientist Minifigs. But what if not everyone on your team is aware of this? Or what if you need to change the sequence and one of your team members forgets that 0 now equals the Deliver Car and Pallet of Power program? Sequence numbers can be confusing to people. When you're running a robot under a high-pressure time frame, you want to make things as easy as possible.

The master program will be much more user-friendly if we add a method that displays the program name instead of the program sequence number. You will notice that in each of the code loops shown in Figure 11-17, there is a Number to Text block used to convert the integer value of the sequence to a text value so that we can display the value on the NXT screen. What if we changed our code to execute a block that converts the sequence number to a string value that displays the name of the program that is about to run?

In Figure 11-18, you see such a program. You might recognize this as the data array from earlier in the chapter. The variable called Sequence is passed into a Switch block that is very similar to the Switch block we have in the master program, but instead of having a My Block for each of our programs inside it, there is a Text variable. Each sequence value will write a text value to the Text 1 variable. This text value is hard-coded so that if the order of the programs is changed, then this Switch block will have to be changed—just like the Switch block in the master program. The nice thing is that when we turn this program into a My Block, you only have to make the change to the code once—and it will update all locations in the master program that the My Block is used.

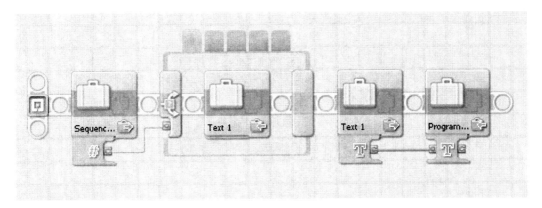

Figure 11-18. An NXT-G program to retrieve the program name associated with the given sequence number

The final step in the program is to write the value of the variable Text 1 to the text variable Program Name. The reason that this step is done this way versus hard-coding the value into the text variable Program Name will become a bit more obvious when we convert the program into our new My Block.

We have this nice little program and we want to make it into a handy Sequence to Program Name My Block. To do this right, we select all the blocks between the first variable block and the last variable block. In doing so, don't include the first and last block. Select the blocks as shown in Figure 11-19. By doing this, the new My Block will have an input parameter and an output parameter, as seen in Figure 11-20.

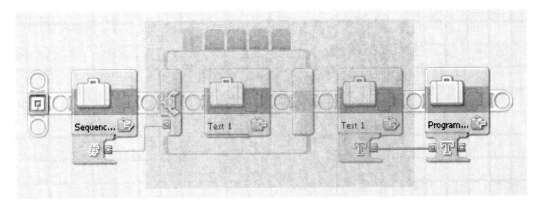

Figure 11-19. Code selection when making the new Sequence to Program Name My Block

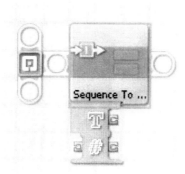

Figure 11-20. The Sequence to Program Name My Block

Now that we have our new Sequence to Program Name block, we can go back into our master program and replace the Number to Text blocks with our new block. Figure 11-21 shows what this would look like. The new block would be used in three places in our current master program.

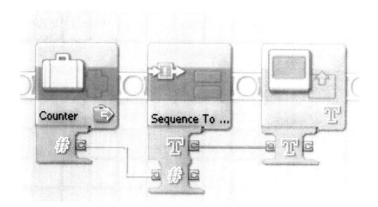

Figure 11-21. The Sequence to Program Name My Block in use

Saving State

Our master program is getting pretty advanced. It keeps our programs in order, has smooth navigation features, and even displays the program we're running (or are about to run).

What happens, though, if the master program gets accidentally shut off? When you start it up again, the sequence will start at the beginning. This isn't much of a crisis since you can simply use the navigation buttons to move to the program that you want to run next. But what if, in all the confusion, you forget which program is next? Wouldn't it be nice if the NXT could remember where it was in the sequence before the master program stopped?

The solution is to save the current state whenever it changes. To do that, we can keep a file on the NXT that stores the value of the current sequence order. So every time we change the sequence order, we update the file by writing the new value to it. Then, every time the master program starts up, it can read this file and remember where it was last.

Figure 11-22 shows sample NXT-G code that will read from a file when the program starts and pass the numeric value into our Number 1 variable. If the file does not exist on the system, then the value of 0 is placed in the Number 1 variable. This program will be available for download to help readability.

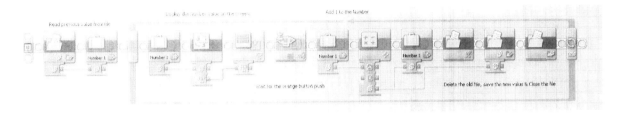

Figure 11-22. *Sample NXT-G code for saving the state of a counter value*

Now the code will loop continually, waiting for the NXT orange button press. This looping is similar to our sequencer code examples. Each time the NXT orange button is pressed, the variable Number 1 is incremented by 1. Then the file in which we are saving our state value is deleted so that we can re-create the file by writing the new value to the file. Before the loop starts over, we close the file. The reading, writing, deleting, and closing are all done with the NXT File Access block.

Adding logic such as this to the master program does not require much effort. It might not be necessary to do, but if you find yourself needing to save the state of your sequence, then a process such as this will work well.

Summary

A master program is not a requirement for any team, but most winning teams at the higher levels have some type of master program. It not only gives a team an advantage time-wise, it shows the technical judges that the team understands advanced programming concepts. So if you use such a program, be sure you understand why you're using it and how it works.

The examples I have shown in this chapter are strictly examples to get you started. There are many different ways to build successful master programs, so don't limit yourself to the ideas given in this chapter. All the examples can be expanded on and built into full-function sequencers with lots of user-friendly messages and quick-use instructions.

Chapter 12

Code Management

Writing code as a team can be a challenge. Whether the team shares a single computer for writing programs or each team member uses his or her own computer for programming, there are challenges in keeping the code under control.

Single-Computer Scenario

If your team is sharing a single computer for robot programming, then code management isn't too great of a challenge as long as team members communicate. It's good to have a program task master—someone who keeps track of the changes and tries to keep the code safe.

"Safe" means to create and maintain backup copies. Nothing is worse than having a working program that gets changed—and the program no longer works as expected. When this happens, it's nice to have a copy of an older version of the program.

Maintaining backup copies are the program task master's job. Other duties include managing which team member works on what programs, and playing the role of gatekeeper to avoid unnecessary changes to programs. It is not unusual for a team member to change a program because he thinks something is wrong, but doesn't realize that he isn't setting up the robot correctly or that he's using the wrong robot attachment. A good program task master is familiar with all the proposed code changes and is able to discuss them with the team before any changes are made.

It's a good idea to create backups after each meeting. By default, the programs are saved in the My Documents folder for the current user. For example, on my computer the path is:

```
C:\Documents and Settings\jtrobaugh\My Documents\LEGO Creations\MINDSTORMS Projects\Profiles\Default
```

All the My Blocks that I create are saved under that directory, in the following location:

```
C:\Documents and Settings\jtrobaugh\My Documents\LEGO Creations\MINDSTORMS Projects\Profiles\
Default\Blocks
```

When backups are made of all the programs, both the \Default folder and the \Blocks folder should be backed up together. However, keep the programs in their original folder. Many teams keep a flash drive to which they can copy the \Default folder at the end of each meeting. They then rename the copied folder using the current date, as seen in Figure 12-1.

Figure 12-1. Backups of NXT-G programs

If you need to restore a previous program, you simply copy the file from the backup flash drive back to the original location. Do not try to open the program directly from the flash drive. Always work with your program in the default location—otherwise, you will corrupt the backup copy.

Make backups of your files from outside the NXT-G program editor. Do not try to use the Save As method to copy a file to a different location. Doing so can cause problems with your My Blocks linking properly in your program.

Multiple-Computer Scenario

If your team members are working on different programs on separate computers, it might be helpful to have all the computers on a single network/shared location in order to save the programs in a single location. To do this, you have to put in extra effort to be certain that everything stays in sync.

The biggest concern is the location of your My Blocks. Even if you save your program to a location other than the default, the My Blocks are still referenced from the system default location. For example, let's say that team member Laura writes a program on her computer and it includes a reference to a My Block called AddToCounter. She then saves the program to the shared drive on the network. Team member Lee opens the program that Laura wrote, but Lee doesn't have the AddToCounter My Block on his computer. His program will look like Figure 12-2. The My Block is displayed as "broken."

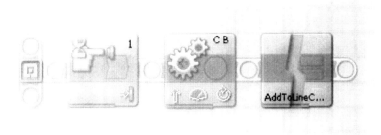

Figure 12-2. *A broken My Block*

The reason for the broken My Block in Figure 12-2 is that the NXT-G program is looking at the data directory on the local C drive of Lee's computer. The data directory is configured in the settings. ini file on each computer—in the My Documents\LEGO Creations\MINDSTORMS Projects\Profiles\ Default folder. If you want all the machines to use the same shared path, then the data directory value on each machine must be changed.

> **Note**   I want to caution you about having all the files on a shared network location. At a competitive event, you most likely will not have any network access. In only very rare situations would you have access to your shared network drive back at your school or home. So if you need to access your programs at the competition, you need to move copies of the programs locally to the computer that you bring to the event. You will have to modify the settings.ini to point to the local location, rather than the network location.

Online Repositories

Saving programs to an Internet-based central repository, or "the cloud," is a popular way to share and keep program files synchronized. There are a few free services available on the Internet for just such uses. One of the more popular choices is Dropbox (www.dropbox.com). Figure 12-3 shows some NXT-G programs that are stored in a Dropbox repository.

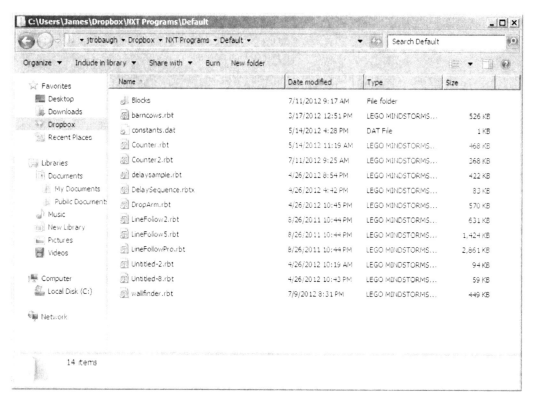

Figure 12-3. A local Dropbox repository with NXT-G programs

The concept is that you will have a "team" account on such a service. Each machine that you use to program your robot will connect to the account via the Internet and synchronize the files in the account to a local location on the computer.

For example, I may have the following folder path on my computer:

C:\Users\james\DropBox\NXT Programs

My local Documents folder is as follows:

C:\Users\James\Documents\LEGO Creations\MINDSTORMS Projects\Profiles\Default

It will contain my settings.ini file, as seen in Figure 12-4.

Figure 12-4. Local instance of the settings.ini file

Inside the settings.ini file, I will specify the data directory path to that of my local Dropbox folder, as seen in Figure 12-5.

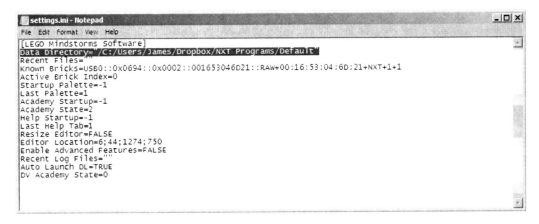

Figure 12-5. Data directory setting in the settings.ini file

Any time that I add or update a file in this folder, the same file is updated on my cloud storage system—Dropbox in this case—and the change is also pushed down to any other computers that are connected to this account. This allows all the other team computers to have my changes on their machines. In return, any changes they make will be pushed to my computer folder.

The nice thing about using a system like this is that you don't have to change your `settings.ini` file when your computer is offline. As long as your folder has been recently updated, you will be dealing with the correct files.

Dropbox (and some of the other file synchronization systems) allow you revert to previous versions of a saved file. This is helpful if someone on your team makes a change, saves it, and then realizes that the previous version of the program was more desirable. By right-clicking the program in your Dropbox folder in Windows Explorer, you see there is a Dropbox menu item with a "View previous versions" submenu, as shown in Figure 12-6.

Figure 12-6. Viewing previous versions of a file in Dropbox

You are taken to the Dropbox web site, where you see all the different versions of the file you selected. Unfortunately, the site is not able to tell you the differences between the versions, but you do have the option to restore an older version and see who the last person to update the file was. Figure 12-7 shows a typical version list of a file.

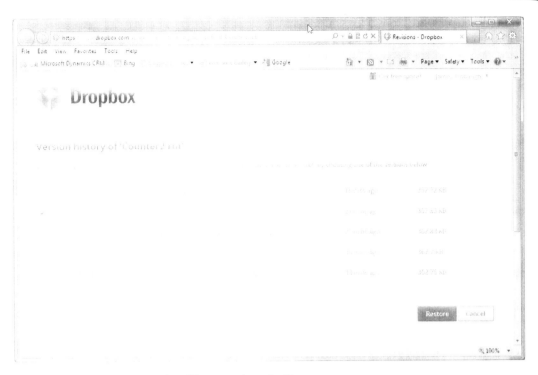

Figure 12-7. *The Dropbox web site showing different versions of a file*

Before you go to an event, make sure that the computer you bring has been properly synchronized because many events have limited Internet connectivity. You don't want to show up at the event with old code. Any changes to your code that you make at the event will be copied to your other computers as soon as your computer has Internet access, thus keeping everyone updated on any changes made at the event.

Team members also need to be aware of who is working on what programs. If two people are simultaneously working on the same program, the last person to save the program will override any changes made by the first person.

Flash Drives

It is also commonly suggested that teams store their programs on flash drives. The idea is that each team member will have his or her own flash drive to save programs. Each flash drive is mapped to the same drive path on the computer, so no matter who plugs in their drive, the data path in the settings.ini file is the same. Changing the settings.ini file is very important; you can run into issues with the broken My Blocks, as we saw in Figure 12-2.

So for example, if my data path is configured for the "X" drive, then all my flash drives should also be mapped as the "X" drive on any computer they are connected to. This can be done via the Computer Management application in Windows, which allows you to specify the drive letter you wish to assign to your flash drive.

In addition to having a flash drive for each team member, it's wise to have a master flash drive that your program task master uses to keep the latest version of all the programs stored. This master copy is the flash drive that you bring to your competitions. To learn more about this method of program management, I suggest visiting www.TechBrick.com, which has a very good write-up on how to use such a system.

> **Note**   Be careful that you don't lose your flash drives. Keep them in a safe location when not in use. It is also recommended that you continue to make nightly backups of your programs.

File Naming

When working with your NXT-G programs, it's easy to want to give the programs silly names such as "Amy Grabber thingy" or encrypted acronyms such as "AGT." These names may be meaningful to the original programmer, but other people on the team may not have any idea of what these names mean.

The team should come up with a set of standard naming conventions. Since the file name is what gets shown on the NXT brick screen, don't make it too long or too confusing. The name should say what the program does. A noun and action can be helpful. Something like "GrabRings" is a good start, but if you have multiple rings on the table, it isn't all that helpful. Changing the name to something like "GrabRedRings" may be more practical. Someone reading that file name will be able to quickly figure out what the program does, without having to dig into the code. Also, if you have combined multiple tasks into a single mission, then you can label the programs based on the mission names. For example, you could name your mission programs "ZoneOneMission" or "DeliverGoodsMission."

Try not to include details such as the order in which the program is going to be run. Names such as "FirstProgram" or "ProgramTwo" are not helpful at all. The order in which you run the programs may change, and the ordering really doesn't tell the operator what a program is designed to do.

Adding a version number is also helpful in keeping track of your programs. Figure 12-8 shows multiple versions of PushCarToBase. By looking at the file name, you can see there are two versions, PushCarToBase 1.0 and PushCarToBase 1.1. You immediately know what the program does and which file holds the newest version.

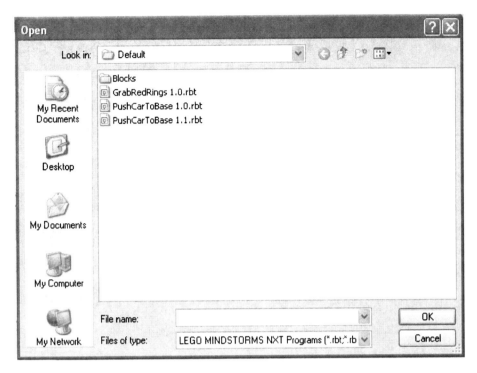

Figure 12-8. An NXT-G file dialog box

Pack and Go

In the NXT-G software, there is a command called Pack and Go that allows you to save NXT-G programs along with other files. Backing up and sharing the MINDSTORMS NXT-G .rbt files is helpful, but extra files could also be required, such as sound, graphic, and My Block files. The Pack and Go command packages backup all the files in your program into one file. Pack and Go files use the .rbtx file type instead of the .rbt file type.

> **Note**   The Pack and Go feature is only available on NXT-G 2.0 software and newer. The Pack and Go
> .rbtx files are not readable by earlier versions of the software.

When you open an .rbtx file, the NXT software automatically places the My Blocks in the default My Block folder, the sounds in the Sounds folder, images in their own folders, and the program in the default program directory. Be careful: the NXT software will override any files with the same name.

To create a Pack and Go package, open your program and select Create Pack and Go in the Tools menu of the NXT-G software, as shown in Figure 12-9.

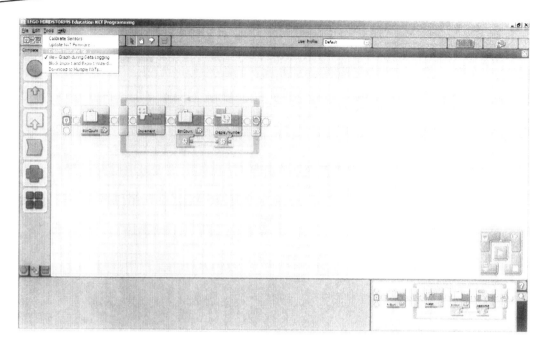

Figure 12-9. *Create Pack and Go from the Tools menu*

Give your new Create Pack and Go package a valid and useful name, and select the location on your computer where you want to save the package. A list of the objects that are included in the Pack and Go file is listed in the dialog box (see Figure 12-10). Click OK to save the Pack and Go file.

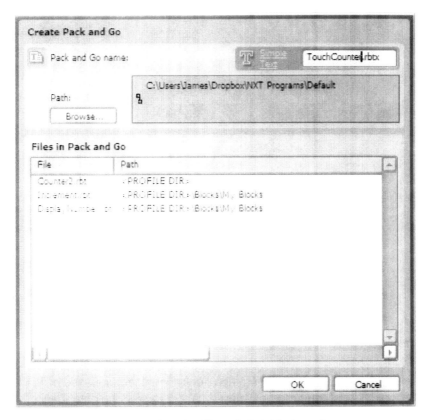

Figure 12-10. The Create Pack and Go dialog box with a list of items included in the package

Code Comments

Sharing program files among team members is helpful, but if the other team members don't know what the code is supposed to be doing, they could spend a great amount of time trying to decipher the code, or even worse, they could misinterpret the functionality and make incorrect changes.

Detailed comments are very helpful in the long run. It's difficult to get people to keep proper comments, but if everyone gets into the habit early, it makes life much easier in the long run. In Figure 12-11, you see a program that contains no comments. It is difficult to understand the flow of the logic.

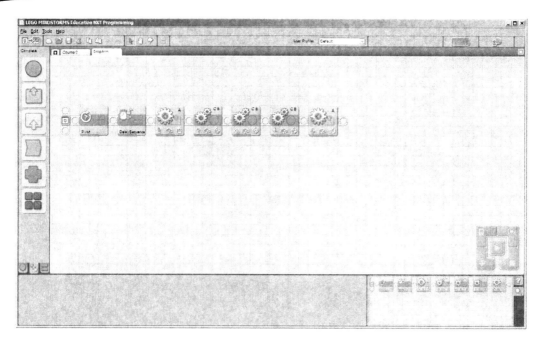

Figure 12-11. Uncommented NXT-G code

In Figure 12-12, you see the same code with helpful comments. You can see how much easier it is to understand the logic flow of the program without having to spend a great deal of time evaluating each block.

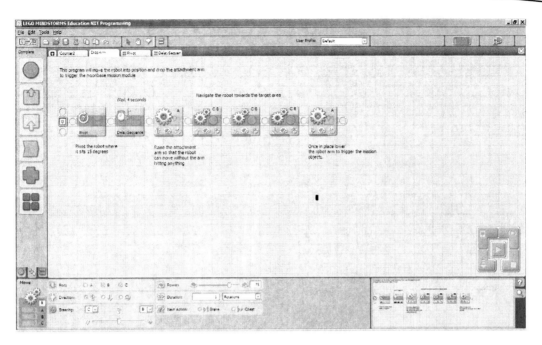

Figure 12-12. Commented NXT-G code

Summary

Proper program management is critical to having a winning robot team. Even though the actual robot design and programs are important, without keeping your programs in order, your team can quickly become disorganized and fall behind. It's important to practice good code management skills from the beginning: use proper file-naming conventions, keep programs backed up, and make certain that you use the latest versions of the code.

Chapter 13

Programming Pitfalls

The previous chapters of this book presented several programming techniques that you should use for competitions. They will help you produce reliable, maintainable, and successful programs that are easily understood. This chapter will cover programming pitfalls to avoid. Awareness of these potential pitfalls will prevent you from falling behind when you are under pressure or on tight deadlines. This chapter and the next (which offers tips and tricks) will help you become an expert NXT-G programmer in no time.

Block and Program Defaults

Both beginner and advanced NXT-G programmers run into the trap of thinking faster than their fingers or mouse can move. In particular, they run into the issue of blocks that have default settings. An example of this is seen in Figure 13-1. The code intended to have the robot move until the Touch sensor is pressed.

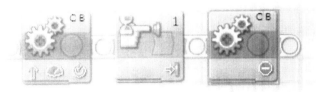

Figure 13-1. Move until the Touch sensor is pressed?

When you run this program, however, depending on how far the robot is from the object that presses the Touch sensor, either the robot stops before the Touch sensor is pressed or the motors keep spinning after the Touch sensor is pressed.

The problem with the code in Figure 13-1 is located in the default setting of the Move block. You see this in Figure 13-2, which shows that the Duration value is 1 rotation—the default when you drop a Move block into your program.

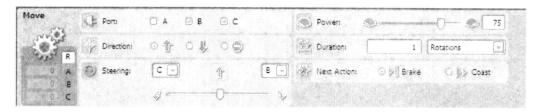

Figure 13-2. Move block defaults

You need to show care with many other blocks that have default settings. Figure 13-3 shows the Wait block default. With Wait blocks, make sure that the default is to wait for the Touch sensor. Always check that your Wait blocks are waiting upon the control you intend them to be.

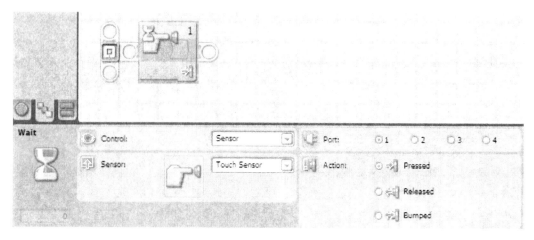

Figure 13-3. Wait block defaults

Figure 13-4 shows the Display block default settings. The issue to be aware of here is that Display blocks default to showing an image. Perhaps you want to display text or a Drawing object (point, line, or circle). Be sure to specify which option you want to show.

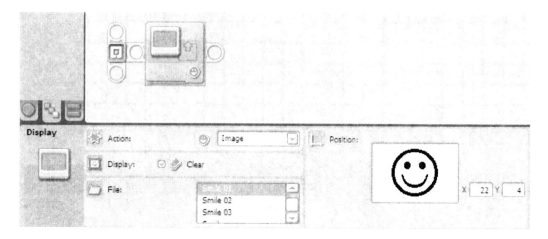

Figure 13-4. Display block defaults

Loop blocks can be particularly troublesome. They default to looping forever. You can see that in Figure 13-5. Sometimes you really do want to loop forever—or at least until some event happens and you specifically execute a statement from within the loop to break out of the loop. Other times, you may want to loop a specific number of iterations, or for a specific amount of time, or until a given sensor returns a specific result. In these cases, be sure that you've configured your Loop block away from the default setting of an infinite loop!

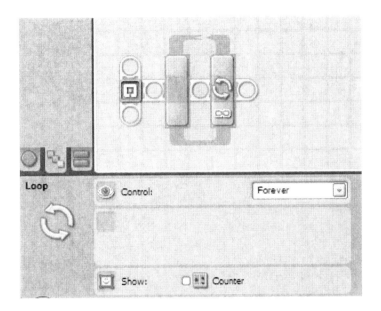

Figure 13-5. Loop block defaults

Figure 13-6 shows the Switch block. It defaults to testing whether the Touch sensor is pressed. There are many other conditions that you should test before a competition. Double-check your Switch blocks to be certain that you've not inadvertently left any at their default setting.

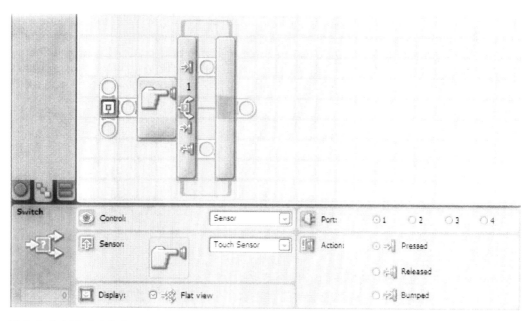

Figure 13-6. Switch block defaults

The Sound block, shown in Figure 13-7, defaults to playing the "Good Job" sound file. It probably wouldn't be the end of the world if that sound were played instead of the one you intended. Still, it might be confusing in the heat of competition to hear the wrong sound.

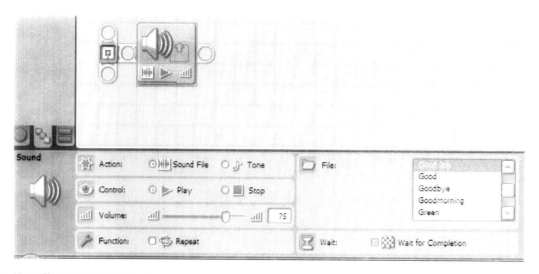

Figure 13-7. Play sound block defaults

Figure 13-8 shows a Logic block. It defaults to an Or operation. If you actually intend to have an And operation, the Or default can pave the road to failure in competition. At first glance, your block will even look correctly wired. Take special care to double-check the operation specified for any Logic blocks in your program.

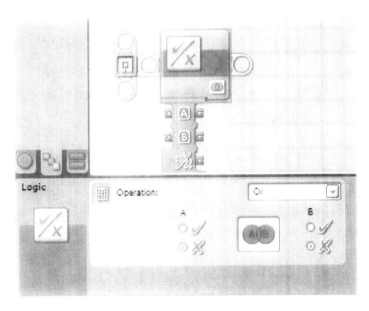

Figure 13-8. Logic block defaults

Finally, there is the Range block, shown in Figure 13-9. The Range block defaults to the Inside Range of 25 to 75. Why that range? We really don't know. It is just a nice-looking range that someone in LEGO chose to use when designing the product. It's probably not the right range for whatever *you* are doing, however. Change it. Make sure to specify a range that works for the program you are writing.

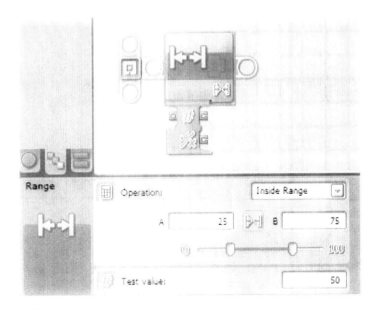

Figure 13-9. Range block defaults

One final default that you need to be aware of is not under a programming block, but is a part of the NXT-G program itself. To create a variable, select Define Variables under the Edit menu. This brings up the Edit Variables dialog box shown in Figure 13-10. When you click the Create button, you will create a new variable that always defaults to a Logic variable, which happens to be one of the least useful of the different types. Don't accept that default without a second look. You will probably want to change it to a Number variable more often than not.

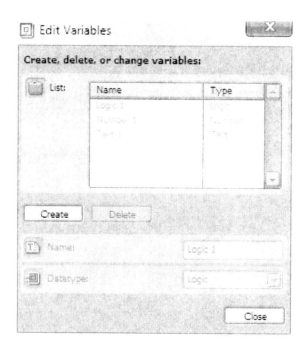

Figure 13-10. *Define variables dialog box*

Defaults are helpful. They aren't all a bad thing. Well-chosen defaults keep things moving and make it easier for beginners to just drag and drop program blocks without being overwhelmed by complexity. On one side of the sword, defaults cut complexity. At the other edge, you can easily default to the wrong choice if you aren't paying attention. So pay attention!

Port Defaults

Likewise, you need to pay attention to the port default values for each sensor to make sure you have the right one selected. Many times, a programmer will think a Light sensor is broken when it is actually plugged into a port other than the default port number 3. The default port numbers for each of the sensors are as follows:

- **Touch sensor**: port 1
- **Sound sensor**: port 2
- **Light sensor**: port 3
- **Ultrasonic sensor**: port 4

Sensors are very important and should be used as much as possible during competitions. If you have trouble remembering these ports, here's a mnemonic to help you remember the port numbers: **T**he **S**ensors **L**ead **U**s.

The first letters are TSLU: **T**ouch (1), **S**ound (2), **L**ight (3), **U**ltrasonic (4). Use the order of the letters to help you remember which sensor defaults to which port number.

The Yellow-Orange Error

Color can lead to trouble. LEGO NXT-G uses color and shapes as means to differentiate blocks. The Wait For and Read sensor blocks shown in Figure 13-11 have similar shapes. It's common for NXT-G programmers to get the two blocks mixed up. These blocks are colored yellow and orange, respectively, so the error of confusing the two is commonly referred to as *The Yellow-Orange Error*.

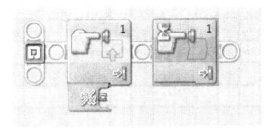

Figure 13-11. The yellow and orange Read and Wait For sensors

The first block (colored yellow) in Figure 13-11 is a Read sensor block for the Touch sensor. Its purpose is to read the value of the Touch sensor at the exact moment the block is executed and write the value of whether the Touch sensor was Pressed, Not Pressed, or Bumped on the output data wire.

If you find that your sensors are not behaving as they should, you might have made The Yellow-Orange Error. For example, Figure 13-12 shows a program intended to have the robot drive until it is five inches from the wall, and then turn left and drive for three rotations. The program is actually incorrect due to The Yellow-Orange Error.

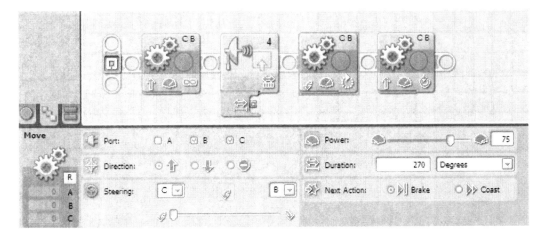

Figure 13-12. Example of The Yellow-Orange Error

The code in Figure 13-12 will actually drive the robot forward for about one second, and then it will turn left and drive forward for three rotations. The reason is that the second block is reading the Ultrasonic sensor exactly one time (doing nothing with the data) and then the program control moves immediately to the third and fourth blocks.

The correct solution to the problem appears in Figure 13-13. The program waits on the second block, where the Ultrasonic sensor comes into the distance specified in the Properties, before program control moves to the third and fourth blocks.

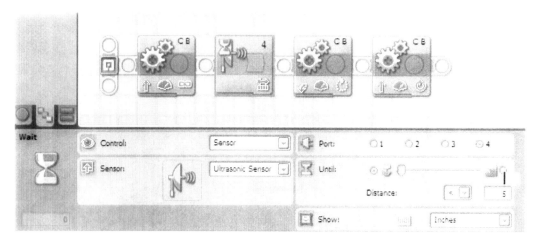

Figure 13-13. Corrected use of The Yellow-Orange Error

Bad Data Wires

In electrical terms, wiring gets old and worn out. You don't need to worry about wear from electron flow. What you do need to worry about is wear from rough handling and bending of the cables. Even with normal and careful handling, wires inside your cables sometimes break. Breaks often occur at the point where a cable melds to a connector, but can occur anywhere.

In NXT-G programming, data wires are used to pass data from one block to another—sometimes several blocks later in the program. Good data wires are seen when the data being passed from one block matches the type expected by the receiving block. Good data wires are yellow (number data), green (logic data), or orange (text data). Bad data wires are shown in the code as a gray dashed line (see Figure 13-14).

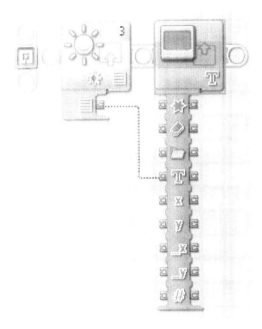

Figure 13-14. *An example of a bad data wire*

Bad wires won't allow your program to download to the brick. You get a bad wire if you try to feed data from one block to another without converting that data to a type that is expected by the target block. For example, if you want to display the value of the Light sensor on the screen, you cannot just wire the output of the Light sensor as input to the Display block.

Figure 13-14 shows such an attempt. It shows a Light sensor output wired directly to a Display block. Figure 13-15 shows the error message you'll receive when you try to download the erroneous program. The error message is due to the bad wire.

Figure 13-15. Bad wire error message

To make the program work, you have to convert the data from the Light sensor to Text in order to be displayed on the NXT Brick's display. If at any time in your program you see a dotted data wire (sometimes called the "marching ants"), then you have a bad wire that must be fixed. Figure 13-16 shows a corrected version of the program.

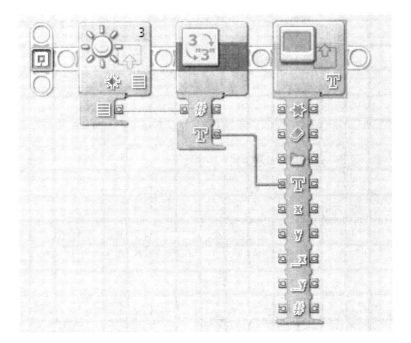

Figure 13-16. Correction to a bad data wire

Use of Stop Block Instead of Stop Motors

Another trap that some programmers fall into is the incorrect use of the Stop block. They make the mistake of seeing the block with that familiar octagon to mean stop moving the motors, but it actually stops executing the program.

Presume a program is written for the robot to move forward until the Touch sensor is pressed, and then it turns left and moves forward for five rotations. Figure 13-17 shows an attempt at writing such a program. The attempt makes the mistake of using the Stop block when the intention is to stop the motor—not the program.

Figure 13-17. Use of the Stop block

When the program executes, the fourth block in Figure 13-17 (which turns the robot to the left) will never execute. It will never execute because the preceding Stop block stops the program and returns the NXT to the Program menu. If you change the third block to a Motor block with the direction set to Stop, *then* the program will work correctly.

So what is a Stop block good for? Since you are shutting the program down, the best use of a Stop block is to exit out of a program based on a certain value or sensor trigger within the loop, while waiting for another value or sensor to trigger the end of the loop.

Hardware/Software Mismatches

Another problem that programmers (as well as robot designers) make is to write a program not matching the way the robot is built. For example, a common mission that robots perform is to deliver something from one place to another. This usually involves loading the cargo on the bot, driving to a location, moving an arm (or other manipulator) to drop the cargo, and then returning to the original point. That sequence is represented by the program shown in Figure 13-18.

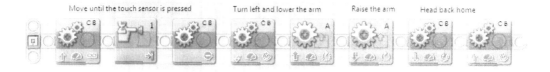

Figure 13-18. Deliver cargo

A problem may be encountered in this example: the fifth block (the A Motor block) that lowers the arm never completes its motion because it is blocked by something (the table, the mission model, or something on the robot itself). Likewise, the sixth block that raises the arm might be blocked and unable to finish its execution, therefore not letting the robot return home.

The solution to the blocked arm problem involves adding another Touch sensor to act as a Limit switch (described in Chapter 9) to prevent the arm from getting blocked. When the Touch sensor is engaged, you can see how far the motor has moved by saving the number of degrees the rotation sensor counted. You can move the arm back to where it started so it doesn't get in the way of any other missions. Figure 13-19 shows this solution in the form of a My Block that you can use in your own programming.

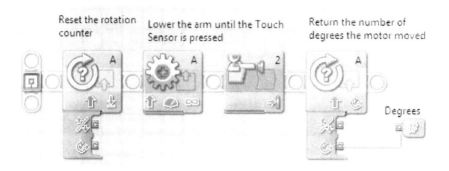

Figure 13-19. My Block to move an arm using a Touch sensor as a Limit switch

It is very important to reset the rotation counter at the beginning of the My Block, as seen in Figure 13-19. Doing so resets the motor encoder value to zero, to accurately give you the number of degrees that the A motor moves before the arm presses the Touch sensor.

Figure 13-19's program uses a second Touch sensor (port 2) to control the arm. The robot needs to be built to allow the arm to lower to the correct position without having the Touch sensor pressed too soon. This is where the robot designer and programmer need to work closely together (if they are separate people).

Figure 13-20 shows an updated version of the sequence shown in Figure 13-18. The new program uses the My Block from Figure 13-19. Notice that the My Block has an output value that equals the number of rotations that the A motor has to move to return to its original starting position. Combining the Touch sensor with tracking motor rotation makes an elegant solution to the challenge of dropping cargo and returning to home base.

Figure 13-20. *The new Deliver Cargo program (with My Block)*

Changing Units of Measure

Similar to the defaults used on most of the blocks, you also must watch out for changing the units of measure. NASA famously lost the Mars Climate Orbiter in 1999 due to this precise issue. In NASA's case, the unit changes were metric to English measurement systems.

As you fine-tune your programs, you may find that you frequently change the units of measure in Move or Sensor blocks. Consider the settings for the two Move blocks in Figure 13-21, for example.

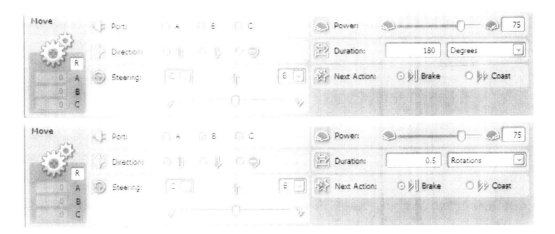

Figure 13-21. *Two Move blocks that operate identically*

The first Move block runs the B and C motors for 180 degrees. The second runs the same motors for 0.5 rotations. Since one rotation equals 360 degrees, the two Move blocks give the same result—a one-half rotation.

A typical trap that programmers fall into occurs when adjusting the settings of a Move block (usually when turning the robot). You sometimes forget the unit you are programming in—and then assume the wrong one. For example, instead of moving the motors 180 degrees, you want to move them just a little more (e.g., 190 degrees). You change the value to 190 in the Properties block. However, you worked too quickly and you actually set the Move block to run for 190 rotations. That's a long distance.

Another unit mistake that programmers commonly make is with the Ultrasonic sensor. You can set it to be less than or greater than a number of inches or a number of centimeters. In Figure 13-22, the robot is supposed to move to within one inch of the wall, then stop. However, the properties of the Distance value on the Ultrasonic sensor block state one centimeter. Obviously, one centimeter is a lot less than one inch—and you are puzzled when the robot gets too close to the wall. In NASA's case, they lost a $125,000,000 orbiter.

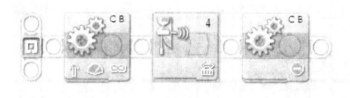

Figure 13-22. Unit problem with inches/centimeters

Work carefully when there are different units of measure such as degrees and rotations, or inches and centimeters. Keep in mind that it's not just mixing up these units that you need to worry about. Be diligent. Guard against this type of mistake.

Forgetting What You Meant

In the heat of the competition season, you will make many changes to the programs that you write. Consider the following scenario:

> What started out as a simple program to move forward for 4.5 rotations, turn left, lower an arm to collect an object, and then return to base changes to a something more complicated as you perform other missions and challenges planned for the competition.

> When you originally wrote the program, as a good programmer, you documented it and added comments to the code. Now that you are under pressure, you just make changes and additions to the program, and you forget to add to or update comments.

> A week or two later, you have to fix the code, and even worse, explain to the judges what the program does. Your comments do not match the code! How will you remember what the code does?

To avoid this trap, always update the comments (you've already added them, right?) when you update the code. Yes, it takes time to do both, but in the long run, you will better remember what the program does and you will be glad that you did the work. Updating comments will also force you to take your time in programming. Simply comparing your blocks with the comments that you revise will help you catch any errors that you might make.

Conclusion

There are several traps that you should avoid as you program your robots for competition. Several are listed in this chapter, along with advice and solutions. Work slowly and steadily to make certain that you avoid traps. If you discover that your program doesn't do what it should, take a step back to see whether you've made one (or more) of the errors mentioned in this chapter. Know how to identify them quickly and fix them. Your teammates will consider you an expert NXT-G programmer in no time.

Chapter 14

Tips and Tricks

The previous chapter covered programming pitfalls but it is equally helpful to have several tips and tricks, especially for competitions. These techniques can assist you with programming and debugging, as well as moving within the NXT-G environment.

Understand Your Program Flow

Understanding how an NXT-G program works with respect to the NXT brick is very important. *Program flow* is the way that a program runs on your NXT, including any delays or changes. Normally, you read (and the NXT executes) an NXT-G program from left to right, following the onscreen technic beam. Understanding each block on the beam is very important. One of the first secrets you learned in programming is that Move Unlimited does not do what it says. Take the following one-block program shown in Figure 14-1, for example.

Figure 14-1. Move Unlimited program

A beginning robot programmer will look at this program and think that the robot will drive forever or until it runs out of batteries. But in reality, the program flow is dictated by a block's property values, as shown in Figure 14-2.

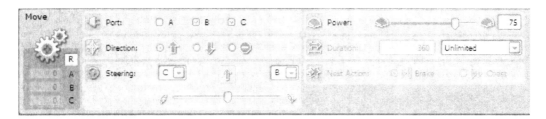

Figure 14-2. The Move Unlimited properties window

An NXT-G program will move through the program from left-to-right, one block at a time, until the program ends. When the program ends, the NXT shuts everything off (i.e., turns off all motors). That is why when you run this particular example program, the robot drives forward for about one second and then stops. The Duration section of the Move block properties helps determine program flow. The program is on the Move Unlimited block for less than one second. Then the program moves immediately to the next block. Given that there is no next block, the program ends.

The Duration on the Move block changes the program flow. If the Move block was changed from Unlimited to 3 Rotations, the NXT will interpret that as "Reset the motor rotation sensor. Turn the motors on. Drive until the motor rotation sensor counts to 1080 (the internal mechanism for the motor rotation sensor is in degrees). Stop motors." Three rotations are equal to 3×360 or 1080.

The orange blocks are a full set of blocks that act on program flow, which is why the name of the menu is "Flow" (see Figure 14-3). Not only do the blocks change the direction on the technic beam that the code gets executed (Switch and While blocks), but they also change the duration that the program sits on a block (Wait block).

Figure 14-3. Flow menu

Your program can wait for a specific time (seconds) or on the actions of a sensor input (e.g., the Touch sensor is pressed or the Sound sensor reaches a certain level). There is also the Stop block, which halts the execution of the running program as soon as the block is read.

Switch loops change program flow by having the program go in one of two (or more) logical lines, and While loops bring the program flow back to the start of the loop. Consider this example, as seen in Figure 14-4.

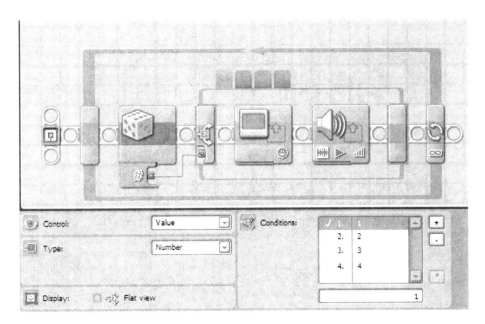

Figure 14-4. Switch Loops change program flow

The program simply generates a random number between 1 and 4 and passes it to the Switch block, which determines what to show on the display and which sound file to play. The Switch block is highlighted on the example to show that there are multiple paths that the program can go (four of them). This program also has a fifth path. It is controlled by the While loop. Once the sound is played, the program returns to the beginning of the loop (the Random block) and reruns the Switch based on the value returned from the Random block. When downloaded and run on the NXT, this program will constantly play numbers and change the display very quickly (1-3-2-1-4-4-2-1) until the user stops the program by pressing the dark gray button on top of the NXT.

Another part of this program has an effect on program flow. It is in the Play Sound block. In the lower-right corner of the Play Sound properties window shown in Figure 14-5, there is a check box that will wait for the sound to finish playing before moving to the next block (in our example, the end of the While loop). This can change program flow by putting small delays into the program while it waits for the completion of the block. So the sounds coming out of the NXT are decipherable—rather than the numbers running together and sounding like one muddled number (1-2-4-2-1 vs. 12421). Another block that has this Wait for Completion step is the Motor block. It will only become active if you choose Rotations or Degrees as the Duration parameter.

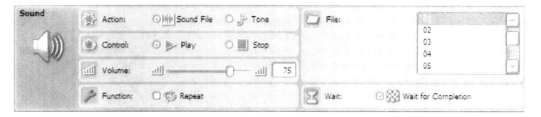

Figure 14-5. Play Sound properties window

NXT-G blocks generally have two items to look for: Action (what will the NXT do when it runs the block?) and Flow (where does the program go next and does it have to wait for something to occur?). The following lists a few blocks and their actions and flow graphs.

Move Unlimited block

Action: Turn motors B & C on

Flow: Go to next block immediately

Move Rotations block

Action: Turn motors B & C on

Flow: Wait for number of durations to complete before going to next block

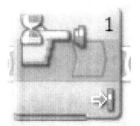

Wait for Touch Sensor block

Action: Nothing

Flow: Wait for Touch sensor to be pressed before going to next block

Move Stop block

Action: Turn motors B & C off

Flow: Go to next block immediately

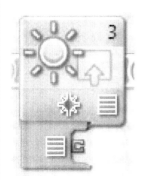

Read Light Sensor block

Action: Output the value read from the Light sensor

Flow: Go to next block immediately

Random Number block

Action: Output a number between the two values

Flow: Go to next block immediately

Manage Your Data Flow

Like program flow, *data flow* is the way data travels from block-to-block by way of the wires that you place in the program. Data flow and program flow coexist without contention. Generally, data doesn't move in a program. Instead, it is generated at a specific time and is ready to be used by other blocks, usually faster than program flow. For example, let's say you want to drive as fast as the value you read from the Light sensor after waiting five seconds. You might think the two programs shown in Figure 14-6 are identical. Let's see why they are not.

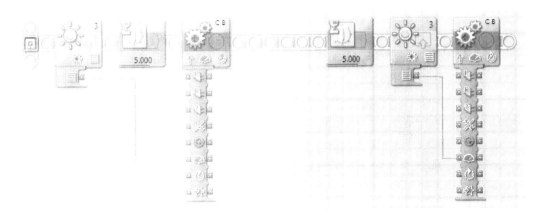

Figure 14-6. Data flow examples

The three blocks on the left side of Figure 14-6 are one way of handling the program; the three blocks on the right are another way. Let's walk through the data flow and program flow for each program:

- The first thing that the program on the left does is read the value of the Light sensor and immediately has that information available for the Move block to use. The program flow immediately goes to the Wait block, where it waits five seconds before actually running the motors for three rotations.

- What would happen if the light changes while the robot is waiting for the five seconds? In the program on the right, the first thing the program does is wait five seconds. Then it reads the value of the Light sensor, immediately sends the data to the Move block, and immediately goes to the next block to drive the robot.

The difference between the two approaches is that the value of the Light sensor can be different, thus causing the motors to move at different speeds. The statement "drive as fast as the value you read from the Light sensor after waiting five seconds" is ambiguous.

The tip to follow from this example is to be as precise as possible when you specify your requirements for writing a program. What you may think is the correct way of writing the program could turn out to be incorrect — so it should be looked at closely.

Debugging Tips

The two preceding sections discussed "how to think like the NXT" and gave you an understanding of program flow and data flow. This section will give you tips on other ways to debug your programs, including breaking down a problem to figure out what went wrong.

Know What You Mean

Foremost, you should know and undertand what you want your robot to do. Write a program, for example, to drive your robot for two seconds, then have it turn until its Touch sensor is pressed, and then stop the robot. Figure 14-7 shows a program that tries to solve this challenge—yet the robot never turns. Why is that?

Figure 14-7. *Drive, then turn example (error)*

Let's recall what you really meant the robot to do (broken down into steps):

1. Drive for 2 seconds.

2. Turn until the Touch sensor is pressed.

3. Stop.

The first two blocks of the program drive for two seconds. But you are missing a block.

What are your motors doing after you've waited two seconds and are about to move motor C? Let's think like the NXT. Both motors B and C are moving, so the Move Motor C block unlimited does nothing. The robot keeps driving straight until the Touch sensor is pressed and then stops.

Figure 14-8 has a fix to this program. Notice a new third block that adds a Motor Stop block after the two-second Wait block. It ensures that the B motor is not turning when you start the second half of the program (turn until the Touch sensor is pressed).

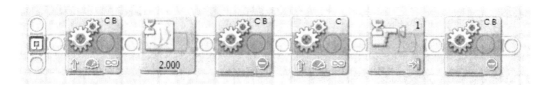

Figure 14-8. *Drive, then turn example (fixed)*

Listen to Your Robot

Another debugging technique is to sprinkle Sound blocks throughout your code to audibly verify that each step has executed. A way to do this is by playing the scale at each step so that you can hear that your program is running in the right order. Figure 14-9 shows the Sound block (and its properties) that plays a tone.

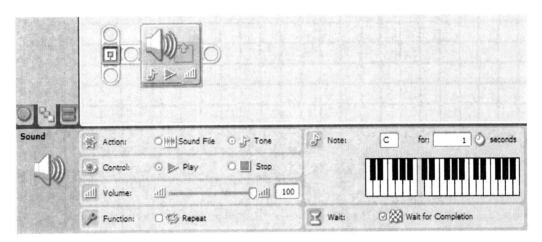

Figure 14-9. *Play Sound block and properties window*

If something doesn't sound right, then you know that you have a fault in your logic. Make certain that your sounds are played long and loud so that you can hear them. Also, be careful not to place the Sound block after a simple action block that doesn't have a wait. For example, do not play a sound after a Move Unlimited because the Play Sound/Wait for Completion may cause an unintended side effect on your code. During a competition, remember to remove the Play Sound blocks because you won't need them during the action, and you might not even hear them over the competition noise and excitement going on around you.

Figure 14-10 shows an example of a good My Block that you can use to help you debug your code. It uses a global variable to count the number of times it is used to play the right note in a C-major scale. When it gets to the end of the scale (tone B), it resets the global variable to 0 in order to start the scale again.

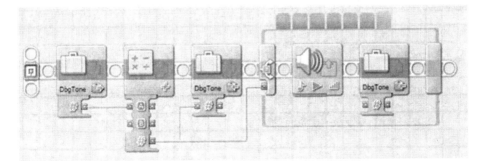

Figure 14-10. *DebugTone My Block code*

Figure 14-11 shows where you can place this new My Block in your code to help you debug it. Having the My Block at various points in the code will let you hear the scale as each step is played. To restart the scale at the C tone, just set the variable DbgTone to 0.

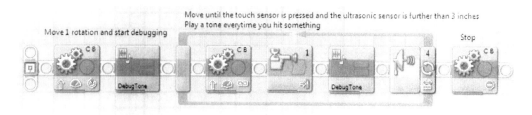

Figure 14-11. Use of DebugTone My Block

Apply Design Patterns

It is common for NXT robots to move wheels for a specific amount of time or move an arm when a sensor is triggered, and then stop. Regardless of whether the movement is driving the robot or moving an arm, and independent of the trigger (time or sensor), you will typically do this type of code in three blocks: Move, Wait For, and Stop. Another way to look at this design pattern is "Turn it on. Wait. Turn it off." The following are a few examples:

- Drive until 3 inches from wall.

- Move arm until Touch sensor is pressed.

- Move arm 3 rotations.

Because these code fragments are very common in a program, we will call them the "Move Until" design pattern. A design pattern is a generally reusable solution to a commonly occurring situation. It is not a finished design that can be transformed directly into code. It is a description of or a template for how to solve a problem. It can be used in many different situations. So the Move Until design pattern can always be implemented in three blocks. Figure 14-12 shows the code fragments for our examples.

Figure 14-12. Design pattern examples

Let's discuss that last block (Move arm 3 rotations). Even though it is one block, it is performing the same as a three-block design pattern. Figure 14-13 shows the properties window of the Move Arm block and the equivalent three-block program (which is not part of the program).

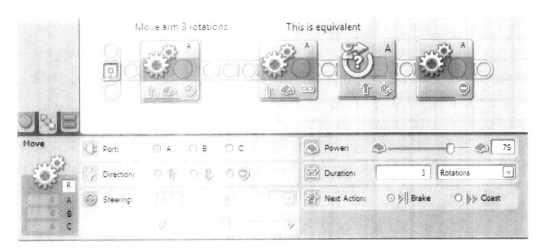

Figure 14-13. One block equals three

In the properties of the single-move block, the Duration is waiting for three rotations, and the Next Action is set to Brake (stop the motor immediately). The single block is equivalent to the three blocks and can be considered part of the same design pattern.

Another design pattern at our disposal is a variation of the Wait Until; however, you are actually waiting for two things at once. For example, you have to write a program to start moving when you clap your hands once, and then stop moving when you clap a second time. Figure 14-14 shows an initial attempt for this program.

Figure 14-14. It's hard to control a robot by clapping

The first block waits for the Sound sensor to be above a certain threshold. The second block drives unlimited until the third block, which—like the first block—is waiting for the Sound sensor to be above a threshold, and then the robot stops. Download and run the program, and then clap once. What happens? Your robot doesn't move at all. You did everything you were supposed to do. Why is this happening to you?

Let's really take it apart, combining the inputs as well as the program. What is a clap? It is a loud noise coming from your hands when you strike them together quickly. But how long does the clap last? Since the NXT can operate instructions at microsecond levels, this program runs to completion at the sound of the first clap. The clapping noise lasts a long time with respect to the robot. So you wait for the clap, but the Move Unlimited block runs quicker than the clap quiets down. So the clap is still heard at the third block, which immediately goes to the next block, which stops the motors and the program ends.

How can we tell? The NXT-G software also includes a data-logging tool that can graph the sound of a clap. Figure 14-15 shows a one-second period of the Sound sensor "hearing" a clap. Time is on the x axis and the Sound sensor value is on the y axis. Let's say we set our threshold for the clap to be 50. The length of time that the Sound sensor registers above 50 is from 0.15 seconds to 0.35 seconds. In those 0.2 seconds, the NXT can run thousands of instructions. That is why the robot never drives and the program ends almost immediately.

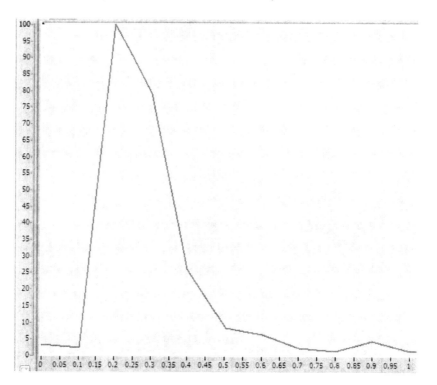

Figure 14-15. The length of a clap sound

How are we going to fix this? Let's change our definition of a clap. It is a loud noise immediately followed by little to no noise, which signifies the end of the clap. In our data-logging tool, the clap lasted 0.2 seconds. So programmatically, we need to change our design pattern to wait for one thing, immediately followed by a wait for the opposite to mark the end of it. The program to do this is shown in Figure 14-16.

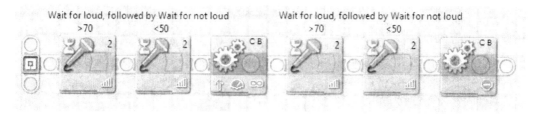

Figure 14-16. Corrected control of a robot by clapping

Now you get to try it. Write a program to measure the distance between two black lines. At the end of the chapter, we'll show you one way to write this program.

Understand What You Wrote

The three laws of programming are to comment, comment, and comment your code. You never know when you'll get pulled away in the middle of programming, and when you return to it, you forgot what you were trying to do. A good way to prevent this is to write a small paragraph that explains what the whole program is doing. Write it at the top of the program. Then, write a one-line or two-line comment around each block or section of blocks explaining what you want to do with that block. Something like this is shown in Figure 14-17.

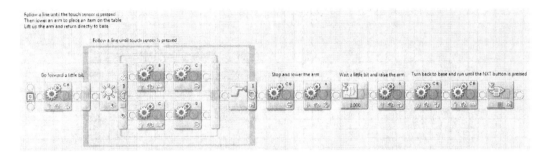

Figure 14-17. Use of comments example

Keep your comments updated. If you have to use the robot's arm to pick up an object rather than drop it, change the comment when you change the code. Don't forget to change the leading paragraph as well. If they don't agree, you'll never remember what you really wanted to do.

Know How to Navigate Your Program

When you are hard at work getting ready for a competition or even at the competition, you sometimes have to make changes to a program rather quickly. If your program is large, you have to find the place in your program where you want to make an update. You will find that you have to scroll left and right to follow what is occuring before and after the part of the code that you are studying. One way of doing this is to select an empty point in the program area and click-and-drag to the right or left, as shown in Figure 14-18.

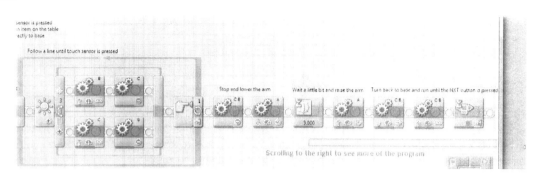

Figure 14-18. Moving around the screen by scrolling

There is an easier way to scroll through the window. When you first launch the NXT-G program, the area in the lower-right corner shows a context help window like that shown in Figure 14-19.

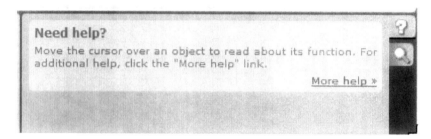

Figure 14-19. Default mode of lower-right corner

When you click the magnifying glass tab on the far right, you get a scrollable view of the programming window, with the current area in the programming window highlighted as shown in Figure 14-20.

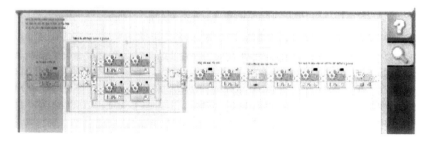

Figure 14-20. Scrollable display of your program

You can place your cursor on the miniscreen and click to have the screen center to where you click. Or you can scroll your mouse along the miniscreen to get the most advantageous view of the area of the program you want to look at.

We do not recommend drawing a loopback to change the main technic beam so that you can see an entire program on a screen (see Figure 14-21).

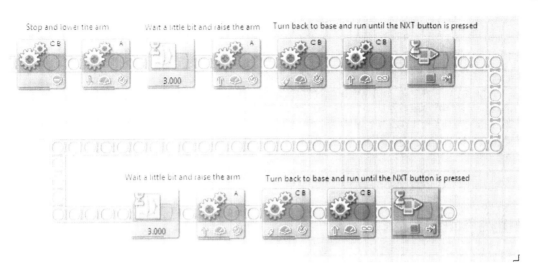

Figure 14-21. *Incorrect use of the main technic beam*

The NXT-G editor may not handle this reliably. You can sometimes lose blocks from the main sequence beam.

Hardware Tips That Help the Software

There's a tendency to think of hardware and software as separate problem domains. This is not the case. Decisions you make in building a robot can influence the ease and reliability of programming that robot. The following sections provide quick tips for robot building, which will help you achieve consistent results from your software.

Manage Lighting Conditions Around the Light Sensor

Ambient light in the facility where you are competing may cause variable results with your Light sensor, even if you are using the "generate light" setting on the block. This is especially true if you are following a line and making several runs at different times of the day. If sunlight creates direct or indirect light on your table, your runs will not be the same. A good way to avoid this inconsistency is to build a light guard around the Light sensor. Add technic beams or flat plates around the sensor to shield it from ambient light. This will help make your Light sensor readings consistent, regardless of the lighting conditions in the arena.

Avoid Pointing Ultrasonic Sensors at Each Other

If you are using more than one Ultrasonic sensor on your robot—or if another robot running near you is using an Ultrasonic sensor—and the sensors happen to be pointing at each other, your distance readings may be compromised. This is due to the way the Ultrasonic sensor is made. One of the sensor's "eyes" emits the ultrasonic wave that bounces off an object, and the result is read by the other "eye." If your robot's Ultrasonic sensor is "looking" at the Ultrasonic sensor on another robot (or a second sensor on your robot), then you will get readings that are not true because the sound is coming from the other sensor, rather than bouncing off an object.

There is no great fix for this, but we recommend that you only use an Ultrasonic sensor in a competition as a last resort and as little as possible. Another suggestion is to aim the sensor down a little so that it does not pick up a direct reading from the sensor on another robot. Try not to aim it too far down because you won't get readings from items on top of the table. If you do use an Ultrasonic sensor, practice for all kinds of scenarios prior to going to your competition so that you have consistent results.

Organize Your Wires

With the possibility of using all three motors and all four sensors on the NXT, you could have a lot of wires going around your robot. These wires may get in the way of manipulators, motors, or areas of the robot that may interfere with how it moves around the table and mission models. Since some competitions forbid the use of non-LEGO parts on robots, you should make one or more containers out of LEGOs to help you organize your wires and keep them out of your way. We call these containers, shown in Figure 14-22, "wire barrettes" because they look like old-fashioned hair barrettes.

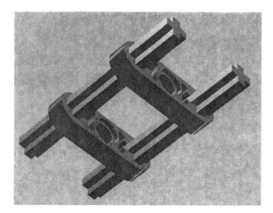

Figure 14-22. A wire barrette

To make a wire barrette, you need two small axles (4- or 5-length) and two cross-axle technic levers. You put the two axles into one of the cross-axle levers and then route the wires between the two axles. You would then close the barrette with the second cross-axle lever and squeeze them together to lock the wires in place. You can find a way to attach the barrettes to other areas on your robot to keep the wires secure if necessary. And you can use more than one barrette around the wires as needed.

Consolidate Logic into My Blocks

You were introduced to My Blocks in Chapter 3 and we've been using them throughout this chapter. Why is it good to use them? First, they reduce the space needed to run programs on your NXT. Memory is sometimes at a premium on your NXT during a competition. My Blocks make your programs use less memory.

Second, the use of My Blocks promotes the good programming habit of writing reusable code fragments. Making a change in one program will automatically update the other programs that use the same My Block.

Third, use of My Blocks makes a program more readable by reducing the number of blocks in the program. For example, we suggest writing a bunch of the Wait For design-pattern code fragments as My Blocks. Figure 14-23 shows three blocks that make up a MoveTilTouch My Block.

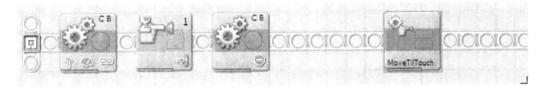

Figure 14-23. Wait For Touch code and My Block

Block names such as MoveTilTouch, MoveTilSound, MoveTilDark, and MoveTilDistance are a lot more readable and understandable than having the three blocks repeated in your program. Name it well, and you'll know at a glance what a given My Block does in the context of an executing program.

Keep Your NXT Firmware Updated

Firmware is the permanent software that resides on your NXT. It understands how to communicate to the motor and sensor ports and how to manage the memory on the NXT. While it is not updated often, it is important to keep your NXT updated with the latest version of Firmware. As of this writing, the latest version of Firmware is 1.31. You can download the latest version from the LEGO MINDSTROMS web page at `http://mindstorms.lego.com/en-us/support/files/default.aspx`.

Don't Reinvent the Wheel

Finally, take advantage of the plethora of software blocks available on the Internet to help you write your programs. Teams and individuals kindly place their programs out there for you to use and learn from. If you do use the code, make sure you attribute it to the author (or web site) to give credit where credit is due.

Summary

Having a bag of tricks at your disposal is a great way to write working programs quickly and consistently. It also allows you to program faster, which may be important when you are in the middle of a competition or under lots of pressure from your teammates. Understanding how to debug programs, learning how to streamline your code, and using common design patterns will help you succeed at your tournament. Keep these tips and tricks handy—you never know when you will need to turn to them to help you out.

Oh, and the answer to the programming challenge for measuring the distance between two black lines is shown in Figure 14-24.

Figure 14-24. Measuring the distance between two black lines

Index